COPYWRITING

by Rayne Hall and
Nicholas C Rossis

COPYWRITING
Get Paid to Write Promotional Texts

by Rayne Hall and Nicholas C Rossis

Book cover by Erica Syverson and Jasmine Bailey

© 2020 Rayne Hall

December 2020 Edition

All rights reserved. Do not resell, reproduce or distribute this work in whole or in part without Rayne Hall's written permission.

British English.

TABLE OF CONTENTS

INTRODUCTION 7

Chapter 1
THE GREAT CHALLENGE: FINDING CLIENTS 10

Chapter 2
YOUR FIRST GIG: GETTING A FOOT IN THE DOOR 18

Chapter 3
BECOME AN EXPERT: CHOOSE YOUR SPECIALISMS. . . . 21

Chapter 4
LET'S TALK MONEY: CALCULATING YOUR RATE 26

Chapter 5
NO TIME TO BE SHY: NEGOTIATING YOUR FEE. 31

Chapter 6
THE COPYWRITER'S SECRET TOOL: ARCHETYPES. 36

Chapter 7
TALK LIKE YOUR CLIENT: CHOOSING
THE RIGHT VOICE. 48

Chapter 8
THE FUN PART: WRITING BLOG POSTS. 51

Chapter 9
INFORMATION POINT BY POINT: LISTICLES. 59

Chapter 10
WRITING TO SELL: AD COPY. 65

Chapter 11
MAKE THEM CLICK: THE CALL TO ACTION 75

Chapter 12
FROM ATTENTION TO ACTION: ADAPTING
THE AIDA FORMULA 84

Chapter 13
THE TRICKIEST ASSIGNMENT: CRAFTING
SALES EMAILS 89

Chapter 14
MORE THAN FACTS: HOW TO CREATE ENTICING
PRODUCT DESCRIPTIONS 93

Chapter 15
THE IDEAL GIG FOR FICTION WRITERS:
BRAND STORY TELLING 98

Chapter 16
WHAT KIND OF PERSON IS THIS? CRAFTING
THE CLIENT'S BIO 101

Chapter 17
INTERVIEWING YOUR CLIENT: PICK THE RIGHT
QUESTIONS, CHOOSE THE BEST ANSWERS 105

Chapter 18
ENTERTAINING THE CLIENT'S CUSTOMERS:
NEWSLETTERS 109

Chapter 19
HOW TO HOOK FOLLOWERS WITH FUN AND TIPS:
SOCIAL MEDIA POSTS 113

Chapter 20
AWAKEN THE POET WITHIN: COMPOSING
TAGLINES AND SLOGANS. 117

Chapter 21
GETTING RANKED: HOW SEARCH
ENGINES WORK.................................... 121

Chapter 22
MORE THAN KEYWORDS: THE SECRETS OF SEO
COPYWRITING...................................... 128

Chapter 23
THEIR RULES, NOT YOURS: ABIDING BY
HOUSE STYLES..................................... 139

Chapter 24
FIND PICTURES TO SUPPORT YOUR WORDS:
SOURCING ILLUSTRATIONS 146

Chapter 25
THE PLACE WHERE IT HAPPENS: OPTIMISING
THE LANDING PAGE................................. 156

CHAPTER 26
THE ETHICS OF COPYWRITING: DON'T DO
A CLIENT'S DIRTY WORK........................... 162

Chapter 27
TROUBLESHOOTING: HOW TO DEAL WITH
DIFFICULT CLIENTS................................ 167

Chapter 28
EXPAND YOUR SCOPE: DEVELOPING
YOUR BUSINESS.................................... 171

DEAR READER 175

ACKNOWLEDGEMENTS 177

ABOUT THE AUTHORS 178

INTRODUCTION

Do you want to earn good money as a freelance writer? Copywriting is the field that pays best.

It can be a lucrative business, especially for journalists and fiction authors who adapt their existing writing skills. As a copywriter, you can earn while you learn, taking paid gigs while you're learning your craft. You can work from home or travelling, part-time or full-time. You can adapt the schedule and workload to your lifestyle. If your book sales plateau or your novel-author career is slow to take off, copywriting can help pay the bills.

In this book, you'll get insider knowledge from two experts. Nicholas C Rossis and I are both experienced copywriters with different specialisms. He specialises in writing for agencies, companies, and professionals, while my clients are mostly authors, publishers, and travel sites. We each write about the subjects we know best, and we add comments to each other's chapters, so you get two perspectives.

Step by step, we will show you the path to copywriting success. We'll guide you on to find clients, get your foot in the door, negotiate your fee, handle difficult clients, and work with SEO. You'll learn how to write different kinds of copy: sales emails, advertisements, slogans, social media posts, blogs, newsletters, bios and media interviews.

Copywriting covers two fields: sales copy and content.

- Sales copywriting promotes a product or service, and aims to bring about a sale. Examples: advertisements, sales emails, product descriptions. These tend to be the best-paying gigs.

- Content-writing builds a brand's reputation. There's no overt selling. Instead, the text creates interest in the brand, showing it to be enjoyable, trustworthy and competent. Examples: instructional articles, tweeted tips, listicles, blog posts, slogans.

In practice, the two areas often overlap, and clients want copywriters who can handle both. That's why we're covering both forms in this book.

You can use this guide as a self-study course in copywriting. Each chapter contains information, professional tips, cautions about novice mistakes to avoid, and assignments. I suggest you read the whole book to get an overview, then choose the chapters you want to study in depth.

You don't need any copywriting experience to follow the instructions, but you need to have good general writing skills.

Nicholas and I both write in British English, which means some words, spellings, and punctuation marks may differ from the American English you're used to. To avoid clumsy 'he or she,' 'him or her,' 'his or hers' constructions, we've used the female pronoun in some paragraphs, the male in others. Everything in this book applies to people of any gender.

We've used the word 'clients' for people who buy copywriting services from you and 'customers' for those who buy products from your client.

Nicholas and I both work as freelance copywriters and simultaneously pursue other forms of writing. Nicholas pens Sci-

Fi Fantasy novels, short stories, and children's books, while I write non-fiction books (including the Writer's Craft series) and Gothic Horror stories.

We both love what we do, and we hope you'll experience the same joy reaping a good freelance income.

Rayne Hall

CHAPTER 1

THE GREAT CHALLENGE: FINDING CLIENTS

Rayne Hall

In every freelance business, the difficult part is getting customers willing to pay for what you do, and copywriting is no exception. But as a copywriter, you have one great advantage: once you know how to attract customers to your clients' business, you can use the same copywriting skill to attract clients to your own.

GETTING STARTED

Hooking your first client is the biggest hurdle. Clients seeking to hire a copywriter want someone with a proven track record, experience and samples of work. This can leave you in a Catch-22 situation: no jobs without samples of previous work, and no samples without landing a job.

The solution: offer your services free to a small entrepreneur, a freelance artist, or a local charity. If they have neither copywriting skills nor a budget to hire an expert, they'll be grateful for your help. Write (or rewrite) their website, bio, product descriptions, blog posts, social media profiles, or whatever they require. Make sure you do a brilliant job, so you can use the assignment to showcase your skills.

JOIN FREELANCE AGENCIES

Agency sites serve as virtual meeting places where clients find copywriters, and copywriters find clients. These are your best source of work and income, at least until you're established.

On some sites, clients advertise their jobs and copywriters apply. On others, copywriters advertise their services and clients respond. Yet others act like a dating agency, matching the right copywriter to the job.

Some agencies specialise in copywriters, others in writers of all kinds, while yet others broker any type of freelance services. The bigger the agency, the more potential clients you can meet and the more potential jobs you will hear about and can apply to.

Signing up gives you many advantages:

- Above all, you'll meet clients who are actively looking for the services you provide, which solves the freelance copywriter's main problem. Typically, they also offer a space where you can display your profile, list your credentials, and showcase your skills.

- You can check out your competition. Visit your competitors' profiles, study their strengths and weaknesses, compare their fees and analyse their success.

- Most agencies provide escrow services. This means the client pays the money in advance and the agency holds the amount and releases it to the freelancer once the job is complete. This reduces the risk for both parties: the client doesn't need to worry about a freelancer who'll take the money and not deliver the work, and you, as a freelancer, don't need to worry about chasing up money from non-paying clients.

- Agencies often have a review rating system, where clients write about their experience and award stars for how satisfied they are with a freelancer's work. When potential clients see that you've tackled similar assignments before and have earned praise, they conclude that you'll do a good job for them, too, and hire you. You can even earn 'Top Rated Freelancer' badges which will make you stand out within the agency. Of course, this works in your favour only if you provide top notch work and earn good reviews.

- The review system works the other way round, too. Freelancers rate the clients, reporting if they were good to work with or not. By reading your peers' assessments, you can avoid problem clients who don't answer questions, change their requirements halfway through the assignment and make unreasonable demands.

- Some agencies offer contract templates, free training about in-demand skills, and forums where freelancers can swap experiences and tips.

Signing up for an agency and creating a profile to promote your services is free. Once you get hired for jobs, the agency keeps a percentage of the money you've earned. Be warned however, many of these agencies are likely to take a large share of your future earnings.

Craft your profile carefully because it showcases your copywriting skill. Your profile text should be interesting to read, but clear and to the point, without gimmicks. Focus on what you can do to help clients achieve their goals, and consider a presentation with bullet points.

Study your competitor's profiles.

You may discover that 90% of wannabe copywriters fail to write good profiles for themselves. Their texts are boring, waffling and vague, often containing spelling, errors, and neglecting to state benefits. Unsurprisingly, these copywriters rarely get hired.

Study the profiles of the most successful copywriters on the agency's site, the ones who earn the highest fees and get the most work. Put yourself in a potential client's mind, and you'll immediately see how these skilfully crafted profiles pull you in. This can give you ideas for your own presentation. Obviously, don't just copy what another copywriter has done, but use it as inspiration for your approach.

Some agencies make money by selling additional services to freelancers: more exposure, favourable placement on top of the list of available copywriters, ability to contact clients directly, more applications per month. All these can be useful, but may leave you with no profit, so be wary. Don't pay for anything unless you're reasonably certain that the investment will lead to more income.

Here's a list of agency URLs to get you started:

- https://www.contentdevelopmentpros.com/
- https://www.godotmedia.com/copywriting/
- https://copywritercollective.com/
- https://www.upwork.com/
- https://www.freelancer.com/
- https://www.fiverr.com/
- https://www.toptal.com/
- https://www.simplyhired.com/
- https://www.peopleperhour.com/
- https://www.writeraccess.com/
- https://aquent.com/
- https://www.skyword.com/

There are hundreds of agencies online. Research their services and terms and conditions carefully and sign up for several if they seem a good fit for you.

Create profiles and start applying for jobs. You will soon find which of the agencies suit you best. Focus your efforts on those, aiming to get great feedback. It's better to be a top-rated freelancer with one or two agencies than a nobody with many.

MARKET YOURSELF ON SOCIAL MEDIA

Create social media accounts, a blog or a website for your business. Although on their own, they're unlikely to bring many new prospects to your door, they work brilliantly in conjunction with other sources. They serve to demonstrate your handling of website copy, product descriptions, social media posts and profiles, and blog content.

CONNECT WITH OTHER SERVICE PROVIDERS

Link-in with freelancers whose services complement your own: web designers, social media managers and business consultants. They can suggest you to their clients, or hire you to complete part of a job for which they don't have the expertise.

Make sure that the people you connect with are honest, skilled, and dependable, because the quality of their work will impact the reputation of yours.

REPEAT CUSTOMERS

The magic ingredient for your success recipe is repeat clients.

Clients who love your work and know they can depend on you to deliver top-notch quality to schedule will hire you again and again.

Cherish them, because you won't need to spend your time, effort, and money on winning new clients. You also won't need to worry what the cooperation will be like or whether they will pay your invoice promptly.

How do you get repeats? Be dependable, communicate promptly, respect their wishes, and deliver top quality. Express enthusiasm for the job, and tell your clients how much you enjoy working with them and how delighted you are to contribute to their project. Make sure your clients are 100% satisfied. If they're disappointed with something, put it right, immediately.

WORD-OF-MOUTH RECOMMENDATIONS

When happy customers recommend you to others, rejoice! This is the best marketing method of them all: it has more persuasion power than anything else and costs nothing.

Go out of your way to bring this about. At the end of an assignment, ask your clients if they're happy. Once they've said 'yes', ask them for referrals. Don't be shy, just say frankly that you're looking for more clients, and couch it in positive terms. "I really enjoyed this assignment. Do you know anyone else needing similar work?" or "I'd love to have more clients like you. Could you put me in touch with other musicians who may need a copywriter? I'd appreciate that."

NOVICE MISTAKES TO AVOID

When you're new in the field, don't simply set up a website advertising your services and expect clients to find you. They won't.

INSIDER TIP

Every communication with potential clients—your application to their advertisements, your e-mail reply to their enquiries—showcases your copywriting skills. Craft your responses with care, so they become shiny samples of your work.

Every communication with existing clients encourages future hires, either from this client or the client's recommendations.

NICHOLAS' SUGGESTION

Coming up with new clients can be really hard. That's why I cannot stress enough the importance of having repeat clients.

A common mistake is to let your professionalism slip with old clients. A day only has so many hours and we have to choose where to focus. As time goes by, we may be tempted to think that we can get away with missing deadlines or offer lower-quality work, saving our best work for new clients we wish to impress.

In fact, it's the other way around. Not only do you owe it to the people who have trusted you in the past to bring them your A-game, the new prospect may not even pan out. You may well end up with losing not one but two clients.

For that same reason, don't get too attached to your copy. This will help immensely in ensuring that you turn new clients into repeat ones.

When I first started working with one of my favourite clients, I knew she had tried different writers in the past. I asked her to tell me what mistakes the last one had made, to ensure I didn't repeat them.

She told me that she had asked that writer to make changes to the copy. Instead of obliging, the writer had taken offence, accusing the client of disrespecting his work and refusing to make the requested edits. Unsurprisingly, their collaboration soon ended.

When you write for a client, distance yourself from the work. You can write your own ideas at your own time. It is also okay to decline any work that goes against your personal beliefs.

What is *not* okay is to refuse to write what your client has asked for, even if you feel strongly that their requested changes will cause the copy to suffer.

That has happened to me more than once. A client recently asked me to remove vital keywords from the copy because they didn't like how the text read with them. I explained that the page's SEO would suffer greatly because of the changes and made sure the client understood that. When they insisted regardless, I edited the copy according to their wishes. After all, it's their website!

If you do all that, you may well find that word-of-mouth and repeat clients give you enough work to keep you busy throughout the year. You will have to spend less and less time looking for new clients and more time doing what you love—writing!

ASSIGNMENT

Sign up with one or several agencies. Write a really strong profile that not only lists your skills but demonstrates them.

CHAPTER 2

YOUR FIRST GIG: GETTING A FOOT IN THE DOOR

Rayne Hall

The first gigs are the toughest to land. Clients looking for a copywriter want to see published work samples and testimonials, neither of which you are likely to have, starting out.

There's a way to **break through this deadlock:** do unpaid work, by volunteering, or as a favour to a friend. Offer your help to someone who has never thought of hiring a copywriter or who couldn't afford one: perhaps a family member with a start-up business, an artist who doesn't know how to promote herself, or a local charity.

Approach them with an offer and explain what you can do for them and how they will benefit.

Let's say your mother manages a cat rescue shelter. She and her small team of volunteers desperately need help—donations of food and money, forever homes for the rescued animals, etc. Offer to write several articles for their blog (perhaps with tips on how to choose the right cat or how to help a newly-adopted cat settle in) as well as social media posts (maybe heart-warming success stories of animals who got rescued and adopted). This way, you can practice writing brand stories (a vivid history of the shelter), product descriptions (a personality profile of each cat), and more—and you can show these as samples of your work.

State honestly that you are at the beginning of your copywriting career and are using this project to gain experience. Emphasise that this is a win/win arrangement: you get experience and work samples while they get free promotional texts.

Be very clear about what and how much you are willing to do. They must not expect you to provide free services forever. Put the agreement in writing to prevent misunderstandings; for example: "I will write five articles for your blog, as well as the story of the shelter and personality profiles for each cat currently in your care."

Treat this as a real job for a real client. Show how skilled and dependable you are and deliver top-notch work. Remember, you're building a portfolio and you want your samples to be as professional as the work you will sell to paying clients.

NOVICE MISTAKES TO AVOID

Don't do slapdash work in the assumption that it doesn't matter for unpaid work. You are laying the foundation for your career, so provide this client with quality work, prompt delivery, and a pleasant experience.

INSIDER TIPS

When you approach someone with an offer, they may voice doubts and reservations. Prepare your pitch carefully and treat it as rehearsal for later, when you will persuade paying clients.

If working unpaid, set clear boundaries of what you are willing to do for how long, and don't let your practice clients manipulate you into doing more than you agreed.

NICHOLAS' SUGGESTION

Make sure that you learn a little something about your clients before you approach them. Tailor your query to their specific requirements. Find out what problem they have and explain to them how you can help them. In short, find a need and demonstrate that you're the best person to answer it. That way, you will always get hired!

ASSIGNMENT

Make a list of possible clients who might agree to an unpaid arrangement. Approach and persuade them.

Continue until one says yes.

CHAPTER 3

BECOME AN EXPERT: CHOOSE YOUR SPECIALISMS

Rayne Hall

If you call yourself simply a 'copywriter,' clients are unlikely to discover you. On agency websites, there are hundreds, even thousands of copywriters. You simply won't stand out.

However, **if you have a subject speciality, you'll stand out** and clients in that field will immediately look at you.

Imagine a company seeking to promote their educational materials to parents who homeschool their children. They visit a freelance agency website, click the copywriting category, and scroll through hundreds of copywriters touting their services.

Which copywriter do you think they'll contact?

"All round writer. I can write anything!"

"Copywriting wizard."

"Novelist, copywriter, ghost writer, playwright."

"Experienced copywriter—all subjects covered."

"I'm the best copywriter—look no further!"

"Copywriter for education and learning."

Clients like copywriters who understand the subject because specialists write much better copy than those who don't have a clue.

There are many hacks who churn out content at $3 an hour by rewriting other writers' articles. They don't understand what they're writing about, and this shows. Their copy often contains factual errors and won't inspire the readers' trust.

Good clients—the kind who are willing to pay well—want a copywriter who understands the product or service, the subject, and the customers' needs.

If you call yourself a 'copywriter for education and learning' or 'copywriter for casinos and cryptocurrencies', any client working in a related field will take note of you and consider you. Sure, those who want a copywriter to promote football matches or deodorants will pass you by—but they would pass you by anyway if you didn't have a specialism.

CHOOSING YOUR SPECIALISM

How do you become a specialist? **Actually, you are a specialist already!** Simply think of the jobs you've held, your hobbies, and other interests. In those areas, you know more than your competitors.

Are you a retired hospital nurse with a passion for aromatherapy? Then declare health as your specialism, and you'll attract clients who sell health insurance, home care services, and herbal supplements.

Do you enjoy cooking, healthy eating and dining out? This makes you a specialist for food.

Are you a pet lover who grew up on a cattle farm and volunteers in a dog rescue shelter? That qualifies you as a specialist writer on animal subjects. You'll write about pet food, animal training, pet insurance, pet toys and accessories, dog houses, cat toys, wildlife reserve, pet sitting services or safari holidays.

Maybe you used to play football in your younger days and now enjoy watching wrestling matches and figure skating championships? You can be a sports copywriter, helping to promote sports events, sell sports gear, and handle the publicity for professional athletes.

Maybe 'gardening and permaculture' is your thing? Perhaps 'cars and technology', 'travel and hospitality', or 'fashion and beauty'?

You may think, "I'm not really an expert..."

But you are—compared to 99% of the copywriters. Unlike most of your competitors, you know enough to write knowledgeably without making idiotic mistakes. You don't need to know everything, as long as you have a sound understanding of the basics and know what you need to research where and how.

DO YOU NEED A QUALIFICATION?

No.

If you have a subject-relevant qualification, by all means mention it in your application. ("I hold a BA degree in Hospitality Management and a Cordon Bleu 3 certificate." "I have a river captain's license, an advanced windsurfing certificate, and a National Pool Lifeguard Qualification.")

However, most clients will accept experience without formal qualifications. Simply mention that you love swimming and sailing or that you're passionate about cooking Asian food. The client will probably ask a couple of questions to ascertain that your knowledge is genuine.

HOW MANY SPECIALISMS?

It's probably best to choose **just two or three topics**, perhaps in related fields, e.g. 'agriculture, forestry and nature conservation' or 'music, education and performing arts.' You will soon discover which of these attracts most business. If one of the topics results in zero enquiries, drop it and replace it with another subject that you may be an expert in.

FROM MY EXPERIENCE

I specialise in copywriting for authors and publishers: synopses and query letters, book blurbs for Amazon, author bios, literature blog posts. A secondary subject is travel—mostly blog posts and listicles, mostly about European destinations. As a German national who used to live in Britain, now resides in Bulgaria and has travelled in many countries, I can write with authenticity about a lot of European destinations.

For a while, I included 'cats' among my specialisms. Much as I enjoy writing about kitties, I found that any copywriting jobs relating to felines were so poorly paid as not to be worth the effort, so I dropped that topic.

I have also written about careers, working abroad, adult education, professional training, permaculture, gardening, mental health, business, branding, and social media marketing.

NOVICE MISTAKE TO AVOID

Don't market yourself as an all-rounder, or you may not get any attention.

INSIDER TIP

Study the advertised copywriting jobs on agency sites like Upwork to see what subjects are most in demand. Do you have personal knowledge in those fields? Then include them among your specialisms.

In the past couple of years, there's been a surging demand for writers who can produce content about cryptocurrencies, casinos and legal cannabis. I know nothing about these topics and won't attempt to write about them, but a writer with the right kind of knowledge could take advantage of the trend.

NICHOLAS' SUGGESTION

I was once researching a project related to job interviews and HR. Something that surprised me was discovering how little the hiring process has to do with people's actual skills and qualifications. The one thing that seems to ensure a hire is **enthusiasm**. It really is as simple as that: people hire those who are the most passionate about the job.

When you prepare your agency profile, focus on what you genuinely feel enthusiastic about. If you love sports, make that clear. If it's cooking that gets you going, say so, and don't hold back showing just how much you love writing about it.

Not only will this greatly increase your chances of getting hired, it will also be wonderful for you on a personal level. What can be better than doing something you love—and getting paid for it?

ASSIGNMENT

Make a list of subjects about which you know more than the average person. Try to come up with ten or more.

Then choose the two or three you want to specialise in. Remember, you can always change your specialisms later.

CHAPTER 4

LET'S TALK MONEY: CALCULATING YOUR RATE

Nicholas C. Rossis

Many writers would rather look for a penguin in the Sahara desert than negotiate their fees. That makes perfect sense. We look at writing as a creative endeavour and not a business one. However, you need to change that frame of mind to make a living out of writing.

Generally speaking, you can charge in one of two ways:

- **A project-based fixed fee**
- **An hourly compensation**

Each of these comes with advantages and disadvantages. Broadly speaking, however, both need you to answer the same question: how much do you need to make a living?

WHAT IS YOUR IDEAL INCOME?

Before you can negotiate your fee, you must have a realistic idea of **how much money you need to achieve your desired standard of living**.

Start by looking at your cost of living. If you need to make $1,000 per week to have the life you desire, then you need to divide that number by the hours you can work each week. Writing is hard and, realistically speaking, you may discover that you can only put in so many hours each day. In our example, let's say you wish to work for five hours each day. With 25 working hours a week, you need to charge $40 per hour.

This is your ideal fee and your goal: to reach a stage where you can charge that amount of money. However, if you're just starting out, you may discover that it's an unrealistic number. New writers often earn as little as $5 per hour. So, would you be willing to work for $5 and work your way up?

WHAT IS YOUR MINIMUM INCOME?

To answer that question, identify next a second number: **the absolute minimum fee you are willing to work for**.

If your weekly expenses are $400 and you are willing to work eight hours a day, or 40 hours per week, then your absolute minimum is $10 per hour.

This is the number you should always keep in the back of your head when negotiating your fee. There may be circumstances when you will accept low or no compensation for your work. For example, you may wish to work for a specific client whom you admire and who will give you exposure and bring more work in the future. Or you may do it as charity work.

However, remember that you still need to make a living, and any hour spent earning less than your absolute minimum means you have to find that money elsewhere.

In my experience, projects that offer less than your minimum fee are not worth your attention.

MORE FOR LESS

There is a story of a cobbler who is looking to drum up business. So, he starts selling his shoes at a small loss.

"We can't afford to do this," his wife complains. "We're losing money on each sale."

"That's okay," the cobbler responds. "I'll sell so many shoes that I'll end up with a profit in the end. It's all about the volume."

I love this story, as it illustrates a trap we all encounter at some point: **working longer hours for less money**. You may be going through a dry spell when few assignments are coming your way. Or you may find yourself with more free time and you wish to spend it working, even if it is for less money.

What's insidious about this situation is that it can be pretty hard to break out of.

To understand why, picture two writers.

One is making $10 an hour. He is barely able to cover his bills and has no free time at all. His writing takes up most of his waking hours. What little free time he has, he spends looking for new work. However, with his work piling up, he barely has enough time to finish it all, let alone find new clients.

The other freelancer is making $50 an hour. She takes on work that she likes but wants to grow more, to a point where she can charge $100 an hour. Since she has more free time, she spends it marketing to those clients who can pay her that.

Now, imagine a client wants to hire a writer. She emails both writers and asks if they're available for work at $20 an hour for five hours a week. The first writer has no time at all. However, he can't afford to say no to easy money, so he eagerly accepts. By sleeping less and working like crazy, he will somehow manage to complete the task. Even though the second writer has the free hours, she is making enough per hour that she doesn't need to decrease her rates, so she passes.

Now a second client comes along and finds the same two writers. This client has a budget of $100 an hour and emails the two writers. Our first writer is now beyond overwhelmed. He's already swamped but here's an opportunity he can't miss. Even though he can't possibly afford the time, he says yes. The second writer also says yes. After all, this is what she's been working towards: getting a $100-an-hour client. She finally has an opportunity to prove herself and, hopefully, land more clients based on her work with this one.

Assuming that both writers have the same skill-set, which of the two is more likely to send the right material to the client to get the job? Even if the first one enlists the help of friends and relatives to create a perfect pitch, which one is more likely to burn out or make silly mistakes because he's working on four hours of sleep a night?

So, regardless of which fee model you prefer—project-based or hourly-based—**be ready to walk away from assignments that end up paying you less money than your minimum hourly compensation**.

NOVICE MISTAKE TO AVOID

A lot of people are looking for someone to work for them for free in exchange for exposure. While there are a few cases when exposure will genuinely help, don't fall into the exposure trap. In most cases, exposure is overrated. If someone is serious about giving you more work, they will be willing to pay for it.

INSIDER TIP

Most people don't realize how hard writing is. You need to leave enough time in the day to recharge your batteries or you may soon burn out. Yes, you will need to burn the midnight oil on occasion. But you can't do so on a permanent basis. In that sense, the best way to make writing your career is to spend less time writing!

RAYNE'S SUGGESTION

When calculating your minimum fee, bear in mind that you need to earn enough to cover the times when you're not working, such as holidays and sickness.

I agree with Nicholas: don't let clients wheedle you into writing for 'exposure' instead of payment. Those clients are trying to rip off gullible new writers.

On rare occasions, you may decide to give your services for free—for example, when you're first starting out—but only if you gain a tangible benefit, such as a portfolio of work samples which you can use to kickstart your career.

I would only ever agree to work for free for someone who couldn't afford the services of a copywriter, e.g. a small charity.

ASSIGNMENT

Calculate your minimum and your ideal fee. Be sure to include more than your bare essentials: life requires more than food and rent.

Next, visit the hiring platforms recommended in Chapter 1, "Finding Clients." Look for assignments that offer both less and more than your minimum and ideal fees. Think of ways to pitch for the latter.

CHAPTER 5

NO TIME TO BE SHY: NEGOTIATING YOUR FEE

Rayne Hall

Talking about money is difficult. The mere thought of stating rates can make a freelancer cringe. What if the client thinks it's too much? What if he think it's too little? What if you lose a potential client because you asked too much, even though you'd have been willing to work for less? What if you get the job but earn only a fraction of what you could have commanded if you'd only had the courage to ask?

Many freelancers hum and haw when it comes to stating their fee, unwilling to commit, hoping that the client will name a sum that happens to be right.

But that's the worst possible approach, because it drives clients away. Most clients have similar fears: What if the copywriter is insulted by the modest amount that's all they can afford? What if they offer too much, and the copywriter laughs about their foolishness in throwing away money? Clients avoid naming an amount, waiting instead for the copywriter to specify the fee.

While both parties dance around the subject, each waiting for the other to make the first move, it's usually the copywriter who loses out. The client will consider other copywriters and find one who saves them the embarrassing phase by stating the fee upfront.

If you specify your fee upfront—showing it in your agency profile, in your marketing emails, on your website—**you become more attractive to clients.**

Sure, you'll lose those who expect to pay vastly less or significantly more—but those clients wouldn't have hired you anyway. When you eventually admit that you'll work for $30 per hour and they confess that they can't pay more than $3, that's a no deal situation. You both could have saved yourself a lot of embarrassment and time.

By specifying your fee upfront, you'll attract only clients who can pay you what you're worth—and to those, you'll be very attractive indeed.

HOW TO ALLOW YOURSELF WIGGLE ROOM

Although I recommend stating your fee upfront, I also advise to allow room for negotiation in case a customer's budget doesn't stretch that far, or they are willing to pay more.

The solution: State a range rather than a specific amount.

Let's say you've calculated that your hourly rate needs to be $30, so that's what you should aim for. But you're willing to work for less, and naturally you hope to earn more.

State: "My hourly rate is $15-50, depending on the type of work and schedule."

Those who expect to pay $50 will contact you—and expect high-quality work. Those who can afford only $15 will also contact you, to find out if they qualify for the lower rate.

You may also get enquiries from those whose budget stretches only to $12, but those who expect to pay only $3 will stay away.

WHEN TO OFFER A DISCOUNTED FEE

Sometimes, it's a good idea to work for less than your ideal fee. Such situations may include:

- You're starting out as a copywriter and need experience and build credentials.

- You've recently joined an agency, and need to get reviews on that site.

- Your business is going through a slow phase. You want to fill the available time, earn some income and build your portfolio until better-paid gigs come up again.

- You want to help a client who simply cannot afford to pay your rates—perhaps a close friend or a charity.

HOW TO LOWER YOUR FEE WITHOUT LOSING FACE

If you've specified your fee and find the client can't afford it, ask what they would be willing to pay.

If their offer is far below your expectations, decline courteously, and wish them well. If their offer is reasonable and you want to take the job, **offer a 'reduced-service' version,** leaving out something the client doesn't really need.

"Yes, I can write the copy for your website for $200, but it won't include sourcing illustrations. If you provide your own pictures, we have a deal."

"I can work for $12 an hour, as long as you're flexible about the schedule. If you don't need it in a hurry, I can fit you in between bigger jobs."

UPSELLING

If you get the impression that the client can actually afford more than your standard fee, aim for an upsell. For an extra charge, you **offer an extra that's of great benefit to the client.**

For example:

"If you want this completed within 24 hours, the fee is..."

"For $16,000, I'll not only write the text, but take the photos."

"The fee doesn't include formatting and uploading. If you want the document professionally formatted, I charge..."

"I can also drum up genuine comments for the blog posts. If you want this service, the fee for 10 comments per post is...."

NOVICE MISTAKE TO AVOID

Don't take low-paying jobs that commit you to long-term arrangements. The occasional quick job at a low rate is fine to build credentials or to tide you over a rough patch. But stay clear of long-term commitments that pay little. You can't afford to work continuously at a low rate.

I've met freelancers who were so eager to get their first gigs that they agreed to work for $6 per hour—with a contract that required full-time work for six months. Tied into this exploitative arrangement, they were forced to turn down lucrative offers.

INSIDER TIP

Make prospective clients feel at ease during the fee negotiations. Remember, they may already feel insecure and embarrassed about their limited budget. Don't mock them for not being able to afford more.

Remain respectful and courteous. Either work with them to find a compromise solution, or decline their offer politely. They may remember you in the future when they have different projects with bigger budgets, or they may suggest you to wealthier friends.

NICHOLAS' SUGGESTION

Finding a fee that satisfies both client and writer can be hard. However, once an agreement has been reached, treat it as sacrosanct. Respect the deadlines and don't ask for more money halfway through the job unless new requirements have emerged.

Be even more polite than usual when someone approaches you for a job and you have to decline because the money is too little. That same client may well have more projects in the future, some of which with bigger budgets. You want them to keep you in mind when the time comes.

Treat all clients with the same professionalism, no matter how high or low the fee you have agreed on. A writer I had once hired for a small job casually informed me she would miss our agreed deadline because she got a bigger contract and would prioritise that instead, since the money was better.

Naturally, I never hired her again, even when I had much bigger contracts to offer.

ASSIGNMENTS

1. Using the hourly rate you calculated in the previous chapter, decide on a free range. "My rate is between X and Y, depending on the type of work and the schedule."

2. Think of ways to lower your rate to meet a client's narrow budget. Under what specific conditions can a client hire you for less?

3. Think of two extras you can offer to clients who can afford more than your standard fee.

CHAPTER 6

THE COPYWRITER'S SECRET TOOL: ARCHETYPES

Rayne Hall

Everything you write needs to match the client's brand voice in content and style. Some clients have clear guidelines on what words to use and avoid, how long sentences should be and what mood to convey. Others have only the vaguest idea and leave it to you, the copywriter, to develop a brand voice.

I find it helps to choose an archetype that matches the brand's image. People subconsciously recognise archetypes and respond to them. As a copywriter, you certainly want people to respond to your client's brand, so use this principle to your advantage.

Below are the twelve archetypes to choose from. The system is based on the work of psychologist Carl Gustav Jung. Once you've defined the archetype (in consultation with the client, of course), it will show you clearly what to write about and how to write it.

1. THE INNOCENT

Brand personality: The Innocent is an idealist, a child at heart. The brand is optimistic, honest, sincere, enthusiastic, romantic, happy, pure, trustworthy, curious, enquiring. It values tradition but is open-minded, and believes in doing things right.

Effect on people: Those who use the products and services experience joy, feel uplifted, and get a feeling of 'I can do this!' Try to create this empowering effect in the texts you write.

Words to use: *Bright, child, child-like, clarity, clean, clear, delight, discover, find, genuine, good, halo, happiness, happy, harmony, ideal, innocence, joy, learn, maiden, optimism, pure, purity, question, simple, simplicity, sincere, smile, sweet, sweetness, virgin*

Illustrations to choose: Look for uncluttered images with simple composition and clean lines. Cute pictures (think 'kittens') can work well.

What to avoid: Stay clear of fakery, illusion and technical gimmicks.

2. THE WARRIOR
(aka The Hero, The Superhero)

Brand personality: The Warrior is brave, skilful, successful, efficient, focused, confident and competitive. This brand provides top quality, fights for good against evil, triumphs in difficult circumstances, and succeeds against the odds.

Effect on people. The products and services create a sense of excitement. Customers feel energised from using the Warrior's product or service.

Writing style: All texts emphasise the high quality of the product or service. They always convey confidence and often a sense of excitement.

Words to use: *Achieve, adventure, attack, attain, blade, blaze, brave, challenge, choose, combat, commit, conquer, courage, dare, decide, defend, destiny, drive, duel, evil, fight, fire, free, freedom, goal, good, grail, hero, heroic, honour, liberate, liberty, loyal, noble, onward, persist, protect, prove, pursue, prize, prove, quality, quest, rescue, resist, reward, right, sacrifice, seek, selfless, skill, spear, strive, strong, success, sword, test, tough, trial, triumph, victory, weapon, win, zeal*

Also use many short vivid verbs, such as *whirl, march, spin, climb,* to suggest exciting action.

Illustrations to choose: Pictures should be dynamic, full of energy, showing people (including the company's staff members) in action.

What to avoid: Don't use silly memes, vague messages or cutesy pictures.

3. THE ORDINARY GIRL/GUY
   (aka the Regular Girl/Guy, the Girl/Guy Next Door)

Brand personality: The Ordinary Girl/Guy is friendly, empathetic, reliable, down-to-earth, sincere, honest, dependable, trustworthy, accessible, easy to talk to.

Effect on people: Customers and followers feel understood and at ease with this brand.

Writing style: The focus is on interactions, whether face-to-face or online. Social media posts use a chatty style. Your role as a copywriter may include responding to followers' comments and encouraging correspondence, conveying "In this company, we understand you, because we're just like you."

Words to use: *Accessible, befriend, buddy, common sense, companion, comrade, depend, down-to-earth, encourage, equal, friend, friendship, genuine, group, have your back, join, like, mate, modest, modesty, neighbour, neighbourly, normal, ordinary, real-life, real-world, share, stand by, stand with, team, understand*

Illustrations to choose: Go for real pictures of real people, for example, the team at work. Avoid stock images if you can get real photos. Authenticity matters more than image quality.

What to avoid: Stay away from anything pompous, and any kind of boasting, and unnaturally posed photos.

4. THE NURTURER
   (aka the Saint, the Care-Giver, the Mother)

Brand personality: The Nurturer is caring, comforting, compassionate, selfless, self-sacrificing, patient, generous, safe, supportive, protective and strong. She is always kind and patient and helps others.

Effect on people: When using the Nurturer's products or services, people gain healing as well as escapism. When reading blog posts and sales emails, they get the feeling that the Nurturer appreciates them.

Writing style: The tone is warm, positive and emotional. The Nurturer appeals to the customer's emotions. Phrase the Call to Action as a gently encouraging invitation.

Words to use: *affection, appreciate, appreciation, care, carer, caress, caring, cherish, comfort, comforting, compassion, encourage, father, feed, food, garden, gentle, grow, heal, healthy, help, home, kind, kindness, listen, love, nourish, nurse, nursing, nurture, mother, parent, patience, patient, pet, plant, protect, provide, safe, safety, shelter, succour, support, tender, understand*

Illustrations to choose: Choose images that create a warm, fuzzy feeling or convey care and support. Staff members should assume a friendly caring expression for their portraits.

What to avoid: Take care that nothing in your copy comes across as pushy or aggressive. Be careful especially with the Call to Action.

5. THE CREATOR
   (aka The Artist)

Brand personality: Artistic, imaginative, unconventional, creative and authentic, the Creator stands out from the crowd. This brand doesn't imitate, but innovates, occupies a market niche, and produces unusual, exceptional work. This brand is often daring and sometimes provocative. and she's never mediocre or dull.

Writing style: Aim for originality and flamboyance. Use twists and surprises.

Effect on people: Readers, fans and followers feel amazed and inspired.

Words to use: *aesthetic, alive, art, artful, authentic, build, builder, craft, colour, colourful, compose, construct, contrast, create, creative, creator, daydream, décor, decorate, delightful, design, different, display, draft, draw, energy, experiment, expressive, fantasy, fashion, flair, frame, free spirit, freedom, fresh, gifted, image, imagery, imaginative, imagination, improvise, individual, illuminate, innovate, innovation, inspire, inspiration, innovation, inventive, invention, liberate, luminous, magical, master, nonconformist, original, paint, pattern, picture, portal, powerful, rebel, reflective, savant, sculpt, self-expression, shape, shine, sketch, special, transform, unconventional, unique, uplift, vessel, vibrant, view, visual, vision, vivacious, vivid, weave*

Illustrations to choose: This brand is very visual, so as far as possible, use pictures to illustrate all texts. Colourful images are best, especially if they contain surprising content.

What to avoid: Don't bore the readers with waffling. Stay away from anything mediocre or dull. Clichés and hackneyed phrases are taboo.

6. THE EXPLORER

Brand personality: Independent, nonconformist, spiritual, observant, harmonious, adventurous and restless; this archetype seeks to explore the world and himself.

Effect on people: Customers gain excitement or discovery (and sometimes both) from the Explorer's products or services. In personal and social media interaction, people are fascinated by the Explorer and his work, and want to ask him questions.

Writing style: Seek to evoke travel, distant worlds and wonders of nature. Where appropriate, opt for a one-to-one voice, like one person talking to another. In social media posts, ask probing questions which make the followers think. In sales copy, lure with the prospect of independence, exploration and excitement.

Words to use:

adventure, bring to light, discover, excite, excitement, expedition, experiment, explore, harmony, independence, independent, journey, jungle, nature, observe, quest, safari, search, seek, sublime, track down, travel, unearth, watch, wild, wilderness, wonder

Illustrations to choose: exotic locations and exotic foods are great, as are natural wonders. Staff portraits should show team members looking excited, and perhaps use an outdoor background.

What to avoid: don't get bogged down with domestic trivia or with lengthy legal disclaimers.

7. THE REBEL
(aka The Outlaw)

Brand personality: Free-spirited, brave, adaptable, nonconformist, impatient, unconventional and radical, this archetype provokes, breaks rules, and challenges the status quo.

Effect on people: Customers and social media followers feel relieved because someone else is speaking the truths they themselves barely dare to think. This gives them the courage to question dogmas and their own beliefs. People are either attracted to the Rebel or repelled, with little in between. Be aware of this, and don't try to win everyone over to the brand. Instead, focus on stimulating the target audience.

Writing style: The Rebel's brand is positioned outside the mainstream. Your writing needs to emphasise the difference. Express strong opinions—but make sure they represent the client's views, not yours.

Words to use: *brave, challenge, confront, contest, courage, defiance, defy, demand, fight, insurgence, mutiny, oppose, outlaw, overthrow, protest, question, radical, rebellion, resist, revolution, revolutionary, riot, rise up, speaking up, unconventional, wild, wilful, withstand*

Illustrations to choose: Look for imagery that startles the viewer.

What to avoid: Don't attempt any hard sell.

8. THE LOVER

Brand personality: The Lover is personal, intimate, passionate, idealistic, magnetic, committed and often glamorous. This brand is focused on giving and receiving pleasure.

Effect on people: Customers feel they have a personal relationship with this brand.

Writing style: Create a sensory experience, evoking not just sights but sounds, scents, the sense of touch and more. Emphasise that the client's products or services are 'premium' and a notch above the competition.

Words to use:

aesthetics, beautiful, beauty, caress, cherish, commit, commitment, desire, flavour, give, glamour, harmony, ideal, intimacy, intimate, love, passion, perception, personal, please, quality, receive, relate, relationship, scent, senses, sensory, sensual, sensuous, tactile, tender, tenderness, touch

Illustrations to choose: All images should be aesthetically pleasing, or better still, visually stunning. This may mean paying a fee for professional stock photography rather than using the client's snapshots. Where people appear in the pictures (including the client's staff), they should appear attractive, well-presented, with a touch of glamour. Portraits of team members should show the eyes, like the person is making eye contact with the viewer.

What to avoid: Stay away from any content and phrases that sound business-like and calculating.

9. THE MAGICIAN
(aka The Visionary, The Shaman)

Brand personality: Driven, charismatic, healing, influential, knowledge-seeking, wise and inspiring, the Magician is an inventor, entertainer and visionary.

Effect on people: This brand's products and services transform people, objects and situations.

Writing style: Create imaginative, inspiring articles which open up new worlds to the readers. Seek to entertain and enchant. If possible, inspire a transformation—however small—in the reader, helping them grow and gain insights. Convey the message that this brand has the power to make its users happy. For the Call to Action, encourage people to follow their intuition or instincts (i.e. to buy the product).

Words to use: *alchemy, cast, cauldron, change, chant, conjure, convert, enchant, enchantment, experience, glitter, illusion, instinct, mage, magic, magical, manifest, metamorphose, miracle, recast, robe, shaman, sorcery, sparkle, spell, spell-bound, spirit, staff, transform, vision, wand, witch, wonder*

Illustrations to choose: Choose stunning, magical images of grand vistas. Paintings and photos with optical illusions can also work well.

What to avoid: Don't include anything mundane, restrictive, small-minded, discouraging, or intolerant.

10. THE RULER
(aka The Leader, The King)

Brand personality: Steady, stable, powerful, knowledgeable, confident, responsible, fair and just, in control, efficient and organised.

Effect on people: Customers often turn to the Ruler brand in hopes that the product or service will solve their problems. They perceive the brand as an authority to be trusted. Especially in situations of chaos and upheaval, people feel that this brand provides assurance and stability

Writing style: Use a confident, authoritative voice. Every piece of writing has a clear, strong structure. Fact-check everything you write, and make sure you use data from dependable sources.

Words to use: *announce, authorise, authority, constitution, crown, decide, declare, decree, fatherland, govern, guard, in charge, justice, king, leadership. lead, motherland, peace, power, protect, queen, rule, solve, stability, stable, state, statutes, throne, trust.*

Illustrations to choose: Select pictures that convey strength and stability. Staff portraits need to show confidence and competence.

What to avoid: Don't use silly memes. Avoid spontaneous outpourings, unstructured chatty posts, and grammatical errors. Resist the temptation to include 'facts' you haven't verified by consulting a high-authority source.

11. THE FOOL
(aka The Jester, The Joker,
The Trickster, The Comedian)

Brand personality: Joyful, carefree, humorous, spontaneous, entertaining, fun.

Effect on people: Customers know that if they buy this brand's products or services, they'll be entertained.

Writing style: Use humour, jokes, playful content, anything to make people chuckle. Spontaneity (or the carefully planned appearance of spontaneity) is good.

Words to use: *amuse, carefree, chuckle, delight, entertain, frisky, frolic, fun, gambolling, hilarious, jest, joke, joy, laugh, laughter, light-hearted, merry, mischief, mischievous, moment, play, rascal, rascally, risk, rollick, trick, try, wander*

Illustrations to choose: Whimsical, funny pictures work well, including cartoons and memes. Staff members should smile or laugh in their portraits.

What to avoid: Stay clear of anything heavy and serious.

12. THE MENTOR
   (aka The Guru, The Scholar, The Teacher, The Sage, The Wise Woman/Man, The Old Woman/Man)

Brand personality: Knowledgeable, wise, articulate and open-minded, the Mentor provides information and truth, and guides and teaches others.

Effect on people: People feel that they can learn by listening to the Mentor brand, so they pay attention.

Writing style: For content, provide information, advice, instructions and insights. The listicle format works well, as do 'how to do this step-by-step' articles. For any controversial topic, aim for a balanced view, showing both sides. For sales copy, emphasise that the product or service will open up new perspectives and help customers understand an aspect of the world. Everything has to be truthful.

Words to use: *class, competent, course, educate, education, educator, enlighten, enlightenment, experience, grow, growth, guidance, guide, initiate, initiation, insight, instil, instruct, instruction, instructor, know, knowledge, lead, learn, learner, lesson, mature, school, student, study, teach, teacher, train, trainer, training, wisdom, wise*

Illustrations to choose: Images should convey serenity—for example, a landscape with an unruffled lake. Staff portraits should feature calm facial expressions. Avoid optical illusions and trick photography.

What to avoid: Dogma, anger and intolerance have no place in the Mentor's brand. Nothing should cause confusion in the prospective customer's mind. Don't tell fibs or fudge the truth.

NOVICE MISTAKE TO AVOID

Don't use a mishmash of archetypes for your client. Mixing archetypes weakens their effect on the subconscious mind.

INSIDER TIP

As an experienced writer, consider using not just words, but similes and metaphors related to the brand archetype.

NICHOLAS' SUGGESTION

Given the number of archetypes, a simple framework may help you better organise the brands in your head:

- **Stability** is the defining factor of the Nurturer, Ruler, and Creator archetypes.
- **Paradise** is that of the Innocent, Mentor, and Explorer ones.
- **Impact** is associated with the Rebel, Magician, and Warrior archetypes.

- Finally, **Belonging** is the defining factor of the Lover, Fool, and Ordinary Girl/Guy.

Focus your copy around these concepts for maximum effect.

ASSIGNMENTS

1. To practice identifying archetype, watch a solo performer—perhaps a stand-up comedian, a rock guitarist or a motivational speaker—either live or on video. Imagine this person has hired you as copywriter for their brand. As you study their performance, look for clues to the archetype they convey: are they the Mentor or the Rebel, the Lover or the Fool?

2. Now consider a current or prospective client. Think about their values and mission statement, study their existing materials, watch how they act in public. What archetype is the best fit for them? (You may notice discrepancies. This is where they need your expert help, so all their copy is consistent with the brand image they want to convey.)

CHAPTER 7

TALK LIKE YOUR CLIENT: CHOOSING THE RIGHT VOICE

Rayne Hall

The voice (tone, style) you write in must be not your own, but your client's, and to some extent, the target audience's.

CONSIDER THE ARCHETYPE

To get the client's voice right, you need to get the personality across, and the archetype is the key to unlocking this. In the chapter on archetypes, I've provided a broad guideline for the right style, as well as some specific words to use. For example, the Ruler's voice is probably calm, competent and authoritative, while the Ordinary Girl/Guy may need a casual, chatty style.

Although not every sentence you craft needs to reflect the archetype, nothing must clash with it.

CONSIDER THE TARGET AUDIENCE

Who are your client's intended customers, and how do they talk? If they're mostly teenagers, then you need to use the lingo of young people. If they're academics, the copy can use sophisticated words and complex reasonings. Texts aimed at subject experts can involve the jargon of the trade. Speak their language to ensure that they understand and feel understood.

NOVICE MISTAKES TO AVOID

Don't write the way you normally communicate, because that's unlikely to be how the target audience talk among themselves.

INSIDER TIP

Observe how your client's social media followers chat online. Their communication style will give you a clue for the right voice to use.

NICHOLAS' SUGGESTION

Getting the voice right can be one of the biggest challenges you face. Some clients have no specific preference about what kind of voice they wish for their copy.

Others, however, come with **very** clear ideas of their desired voice. They won't be happy until you exactly match that voice—even though they are rarely able to actually describe it.

If you find yourself struggling with such a project, you have two options.

The first is to ask them for an alternative arrangement. For example, you may write a draft copy in a voice as close to their own. It will then be their responsibility to edit until it matches the exact tone they want. You may even offer a discount if they accept this, as you will save plenty of time—time you can spend on other projects.

Your second option is to simply excuse yourself from the project. When someone hires you, it will be because they have seen your work and like your voice. If they don't, then you may save both yourself and your client a lot of time and energy if they seek a better match.

Ideally, though, don't send them away. Instead, acknowledge that their interests may be better served by another writer and **recommend someone specific**. Or, if you worry that the client will react poorly to this, simply hire that second writer yourself and pay them with the money you would have got. That way, when that other writer also struggles with a project, they will consider passing it off to you.

Writing is solitary work. Forming a network of writer friends who can help each other can be one of the more satisfying things you can do in your professional life!

ASSIGNMENT

Choose a current client (or one you'd like to land). Identify this client's target audience and archetype. What voice will be best for this? Describe the ideal voice. For example, 'authoritative, to the point, informative, using industry jargon' or 'lush, effusive, emotional, personal, rich in descriptions.'

CHAPTER 8

THE FUN PART: WRITING BLOG POSTS

Nicholas C Rossis

Blog posts are my favourite kind of copywriting. Not only are they fun to write, but they are also incredibly diverse. I have prepared and uploaded posts for dozens of clients, learning in the process about a stunning range of subjects, from how to move a tree to taking wedding photos, living soil supplements, the technology of artificial limbs, and house emergency mitigation services.

I have written posts for most kinds of professionals or organisations, from doctors, clinics, and hospitals, to schools, hotels, lawyers, realtors, plumbers, and builders.

While I love the variety, I have also specialised in certain subjects. For example, I have written around half a million words on the medical uses of cannabidiol (CBD), interviewing medical professionals in the process and consulting hundreds of studies.

For someone like me, getting paid to research and write is a dream-come-true. Not everyone's a self-confessed geek, though. And it can be pretty hard to come up with novel ideas for a blog post that both use the necessary keywords and make for great reading.

If you ever get stuck in a rut or need a fresh perspective, here are some different types of blog posts to choose from.

HOW TO/TUTORIALS/TIPS AND ADVICE

How to write, how to promote, how to market… you get the idea. Most people search for something because they have a question and need an answer. Why not provide one in a step-by-step post that walks them through a solution?

Some clients may be wary of this kind of post, thinking that the reader will prefer to go it alone instead of hiring them. However, tutorials establish a client's credibility and expertise. And most people will prefer hiring someone to do the work after seeing how time-consuming it can be. Even if they don't, they will consider your client an expert and may hire them in the future.

DEFINITION POSTS

A variation of the above, definition posts also answer questions. Compared to tutorials, though, they offer a bonus advantage, in the form of **Google's answers**.

You may have noticed that asking Google a question often results in a short answer. These are taken from web copy and blog posts. If you format your copy the right way, you have a great chance of ending up with a popular post that benefits from Google sending people your way.

LISTICLES

Listicles have their own chapter but are worth a mention here, too. Generally speaking, they consist of bullet points that are easy to read. Most people just glance through a listicle to get the gist of it and only pause to learn more when something catches their eye. Easy to read and write, listicles are the chips of blog posts, complete with ketchup on the side. There are many reasons for their popularity, but check out their disadvantages in the relevant chapter.

Give your listicles substance by including valuable resources which your audience might need. This will encourage them to both spend more time on the post and bookmark it for future reference.

STORIES

We're storytellers.

Not just us, writers. I mean everyone. Our entire species consists of storytellers and audiences. Everyone loves a good story.

Use this simple fact in your blog posts. In my experience, few promotions work better than telling a story. You may want to write a short story, a little poem, a little adventure you had. Personalising a post with an anecdote is a wonderful way to illustrate a point.

Stories work their magic in many ways:

- They give readers a sense of the blog's writing, style, and themes.
- They offer a personal touch to your post.
- They provide a change from the usual things you might find in a blog.
- They are original art.
- For us authors, they are a perfect way to connect with our readers.

PERSONAL

Writing a personal post for a client is pretty hard. It has to match the client's voice and is closer to ghostwriting than copywriting.

Even so, this kind of post adds a wonderfully personal touch to a blog and is often wildly popular.

On a business level, personal posts humanise a brand and can be remarkably effective in online reputation management (ORP) scenarios.

If you want to explore this avenue further, there's a book in the Writer's Craft series: *Ghostwriting* by Rayne Hall and Mariana Sabino, which will teach you the craft and business of this trade.

INSPIRING POSTS

People want to see that the people behind a company are normal human beings with a personality. While a personal post may be hard to write, an inspiring one is much easier and largely accomplishes the same goals.

Inspirational posts may include famous sayings and quotes, personal feelings, and achievements.

INTERVIEWS

You may be surprised by how many famous people you and your friends know. It's just that few ever connect the dots to recognise this fact—and do something about it. Have your client ask around the office for ideas on celebrities to interview, and you'll soon be able to write up an interview. As a bonus, it may well be with one of your personal heroes!

CONTROVERSIAL

Personally, I avoid controversy, as it's much easier to taint a brand than to build one. Having some extra clicks is rarely worth the risk.

Even so, there are circumstances when your client wants you to write a controversial post. If that's the case, "sandwich" the controversy:

- Start by clearly stating your stance.
- Continue by offering arguments **against** your stance.
- Next, argue **in favour** of your stance.

- Explain in your conclusion, why the arguments in favour outweigh the ones against it, while accepting that not everyone will agree with you.

The crucial segment of your post is the second one—and the one which most writers miss. It acknowledges this as a controversial topic and recognises that many readers will feel differently. People often react in a rage, especially online, when someone challenges their beliefs. You pre-empt such angry responses by arguing their points on their behalf early on. That will save you a few angry comments and, possibly, a therapist bill.

While you should always be courteous in your posts, civility is twice as important in a controversial context.

SERIES POST

Blogs that have a repetitive frequency in their posts encourage readers to come back. It is best if you can publish a certain kind of post on a regular day, even at a regular time. Make the Sunday post, the weekly review post, or the interview of the month a staple, and people will make your blog part of their schedule.

REVIEWS

Dedicated review sites are popular, with online reviews taking the place of word-of-mouth. They are not the only place where you can publish a review, though.

Review books you have read, a film you watched, or a show you attended. As long as the topic is relevant to the theme of the blog you're writing for, this is a perfectly valid choice. From an SEO point-of-view, a review brings extra traffic to the blog because it expands your readership to include everyone who's interested in said book or film. And if you're really lucky, the book's or film's own social media may share your review, thus sending people your way and increasing your traffic.

NOVICE MISTAKE TO AVOID

As a rule, avoid discussing politics or religion on a blog post, unless your client is, say, a local politician. Not only are these contentious issues, but we also live in a polarised era. There is little point in writing about these unless something huge has happened.

If you do write about these, acknowledge this as a contentious issue and handle it appropriately. Always be courteous to the "other side!"

INSIDER TIP

Here are some things I've learned through the years:

People appreciate a chuckle: a funny image, a comic that illustrates your point, a funny story. Everyday life is serious enough, so funny things relieve some of the day's tension.

Something only tangentially related to core subject: it just rounds up the client's blog's personality and brings out your multifaceted self. This can do wonders for a business brand.

Personal experience and anecdotes: People respond to both a brand's successes and failures. Share your client's joy at winning a competition, his hopes at entering one, or his disappointment on losing one.

Helping others: apart from good Karma, helping others will always be reciprocated, at the most unexpected of times, so keep doing it!

RAYNE'S COMMENT

Blog posts are among my favourite writing assignments, too. I write about travel, horror, literature, publishing, writing, the arts, folklore, mental health and cats. Most clients hire me for advice/instruction articles or 'listicle' type blog posts. A few want personal experiences or opinion pieces.

My only regret is that many clients don't mention my name, but pass the blog posts off as their own work. In this situation, my role is that of a ghostwriter. This is a legitimate arrangement, but I find it less satisfying than when the articles appear under my own name.

That's why I have two different rates for blog posts. If a piece will be published under someone else's name, I charge twice as much.

Be careful about writing reviews for money, because most gigs for review writing are unethical. Clients want you to pretend that you're a happy customer, praising a product you've never used, to help deceive innocent people and trick them into buying. Of course, there's no reason why you shouldn't write a genuine review for a blog, but honest review assignments are rare.

ASSIGNMENT

The following are the most popular types of blogs, listed in order of popularity:

- Fashion blogs
- Food blogs
- Travel Blogs
- Music Blogs
- Lifestyle Blogs
- Fitness Blogs
- DIY Blogs
- Sports Blogs

Choose a topic that interests you and write a blog post for any of the above. Consider offering it as a free guest post to a blogger, which will provide you with a published work sample to show to prospective clients.

OPTIONAL ASSIGNMENT

My author blog (nicholasrossis.me) is on book marketing, writing, and history. Choose a relevant topic that interests you and write a guest post. Contact me through my blog (https://nicholasrossis.me/blog/)mentioning you have read our book and I will consider publishing your post as a guest post. This will help you build your portfolio and get you started on your copywriting journey!

CHAPTER 9

INFORMATION POINT BY POINT: LISTICLES

Nicholas C Rossis

As the name suggests, listicles are **articles in the forms of lists**. We also mention them in "Writing Ad Copy" from the point of view of writing listicle headlines, but this chapter examines them in detail.

WHAT ARE THEY?

At their most effective, listicles are made up of a simple structure:

Number + Noun + Personal Pronoun + Modal.

For example: "9 Reasons You Should Wake Up Earlier."

However, a simpler form like "The Top-9 Restaurants in Ouray" is also a listicle.

Listicles are wildly popular online. Buzzfeed, the 47th most popular website in the US, uses them regularly: a whopping **65% of its viral articles are listicles**. When you start looking for listicles, you will notice them everywhere: a large percentage of any search result will be listicles. And social media are filled with them.

This is because listicles have several significant advantages over long-copy articles.

ADVANTAGES FOR READERS

To the reader, listicles are appealing because:

- **Numbers attract the eye**. They explain right away what users will get. At a time when everyone is busy, they let readers estimate how long they'll need to finish an article. This predictability makes it easier for readers to invest their time in them.

- **They use a simple format.** Most articles have an introduction, large body for the bulk of content organised in clear sections, and a conclusion. This clear structure makes them more readable.

- **They save readers time.** Impatient readers can just skim through, taking in just the highlights. The very format of a listicle makes this reading behaviour easy—indeed, it encourages it.

- **They are memorable.** Lists categorise topics in a way that is natural to the human brain. We all like to see logical progression and systematic organization. Listicles make it far easier to understand and remember our content.

- **They stay focused.** Whereas a long article may go off on a tangent every now and then, listicles are short and sweet.

- **Their content is easily shareable.** Long copy can make it harder for someone to share an article, as they have to pinpoint the section that is of interest to them and their friends. Listicles, however, are focused around a single point, therefore need far less explanation.

- **They naturally generate conversation and engagement.** Since they are more focused and clearly organised, people will easily find something that prompts a response.

ADVANTAGES FOR WRITERS

Listicles offer several advantages for writers, too:

- They're **easy to plan and write**. This saves writers time, letting them increase their productivity.

- Each item written feels like an **achievement**. This helps motivate you to finish the article, especially if you're dealing with a difficult subject or one that doesn't interest you all that much.

- Lists are great for **targeting core keywords**. For SEO copywriters, this is of paramount importance. It can be hard to add certain keywords, especially long-tail ones, to our copy. Listicles can help us with that, since each section can contain the same keywords without the reader perceiving the text as repetitive.

- **Updates** are easier to make. The clear organization and structure of listicles makes it far easier to make an update or a quick edit.

DISADVANTAGES

There's no denying the advantages of listicles. Personally, however, I rarely use them in my copy: **less than 1% of my copy is in the form of listicles.**

This is because of one major drawback: ironically enough, **listicles are a victim of their own success.**

Since they are easy to write, most amateur copywriters start with them. The result is a market that is flooded with listicles, to the point that anything that is **not** a listicle starts feeling like a breath of fresh air.

Partly for the same reason, **listicles are associated with poor-quality copy** in the minds of many readers. A common trend in low-quality websites is to entice readers with a clickbait title. When hapless readers do click, they are taken to a page that has one paragraph of actual text and tons of Ads. To continue reading, they then have to click on a big "Next" button… again and again, for dozens of pages, each of them with a sentence or two.

If you find this annoying, you're not the only one. And since listicles are commonly used in clickbait titles, readers often avoid them altogether.

Accordingly, some clients may consider listicles lazy, low-quality material and frown upon their use. They expect a well-paid, professional copywriter to do better than that. By suggesting a listicle as a topic, you run the risk of being perceived as an amateur writer. It is no surprise, then, that many professional copywriters only use them sparingly.

NOVICE MISTAKE TO AVOID

Depending on the medium, listicles may be gold—or coal. You have to "read the room" to determine if listicles are the way to go with a certain client. For example, a bed-and-breakfast may welcome an enthusiastic list of the top-10 local attractions. On the other hand, a lawyer looking for legal copy for their website or a doctor who shares only medical articles on her practice's blog, would be better served with long copy.

The most important mistake to avoid is to conform to the low-quality expectation many have of listicles. If you write a listicle, be sure to make it exceptionally well-written. You are using a form that is associated with poor-quality posts, so you have to go the extra mile to ensure that your readers (and clients) are satisfied by your copy.

INSIDER TIP

When writing a listicle, **odd numbers** tend to fare better than even ones. Certain numbers, such seven, nine, and eleven, are considered especially attractive numbers for listicles and tend to generate more clicks.

RAYNE'S COMMENT

I enjoy writing listicles—they come natural to me.

However, there's a dilemma when the client requests to include a specific item in a list of 'best' things. Should you include something you don't personally know?

If the client asks for 'The 10-Most Beautiful Cities in Europe' you can probably research that without difficulty. But how about 'The 10 Best Restaurants in Stockholm' if you've tried only five? Sure, you could go by other writers' reviews, but those may also be copied from somewhere else, and the facts get more distorted with every rewrite.

Also bear in mind that people will make decisions based on your recommendations. If your client wants you to write a listicle 'The 10 Most Exciting Rap Songs of the Year' and include his own as the Number One, there's probably no harm done. But how about 'The 10 Safest Car Seats for Children'—would you really want that responsibility?

Another observation: Some clients want their listicles to outdo all other listicles by sheer number. If their competitors publish 'The 10 Best' of anything, they want you to write 'The 20 Best'—and this escalates into a ridiculous race for quantity. I've been asked to write listicles with 50 or 100 items, simply because the clients wanted to outdo their competition. From the reader's perspective, listicles are most useful if the options are narrowed down to a few items that are truly the best.

ASSIGNMENT

Choose a subject that interests you, perhaps one you want to specialise in. Write up to 300 words in both long-copy and listicle form. What was different between the two forms from the point of view of writing them? Which was easier and which was harder?

Now, read again the two versions and compare them from the point of view of a reader. Which was easier and which was harder to read?

Keep those two articles. You can use them as samples to show to prospective clients.

CHAPTER 10

WRITING TO SELL: AD COPY

Nicholas C Rossis

Some platforms, such as Facebook, blogs, and LinkedIn, allow long copy. Others, like Google or Twitter, only leave enough space for a few words.

In both cases, you have to make sure that the words you choose are the perfect ones for the job. Here are some tips to help you write the perfect Ad copy.

INCLUDE YOUR KEYWORDS

Search engines work by identifying specific keywords and showing your Ad copy to people looking for them. For example, you may want your Google Ad or sponsored blog post to appear whenever someone searches Google for "wireless speakers."

To achieve that, you must include your main keywords in your copy—in this case, "wireless speakers." Google will display your Ad more often for those keywords and your client's advertising costs will be lower. And if your blog post shows up on the search page, even better!

FOLLOW THE RULES

Sometimes, copywriters can be too smart for their own good. It makes sense that you may wish for an original way to discuss Bluetooth speakers after writing thousands of words about them. But you must still adhere to the search engines' guidelines.

In Google, for example, tHiS iSnT aLlOwEd.

As for platforms like Amazon, they are even stricter and will often reject any Ad that mentions the number of reviews or includes exclamation marks and non-standard characters such as asterisks.

To save yourself a lot of time, read up on each platform's guidelines before even starting on the Ad copy!

TELL A STORY

The best Ad copy tells a story. Most writers are familiar with the importance of cramming an entire story into a line or two.

Consider this book tagline:

"Whom would you choose to save—your wife or your daughter?"

While it may not be possible to create a Sophie's Choice kind of tension in your Ad, you still need to capture the viewer's eye and make them want to find out more.

Do so by selling an experience; not a product or service. Explain what people will gain by buying the product, how it will improve their lives, and what their "happily ever after" will be.

ANSWER PEOPLE'S NEEDS

All products exist because they answer some need.

The best way to write Ad copy is to identify that need and explain how the advertised product answers it (ideally by telling a story).

People click on Ads because they have a problem and expect a solution from the promoted product. When possible, include in your Ad copy both the problem and the solution.

In the above example, why do people need a Bluetooth speaker? To listen to music, obviously. But that's not all. Think about their story and their need. Who is your target group? Imagine them in as much detail as possible.

Bluetooth speakers are usually paired with mobile phones. If someone wants to listen to music on their own, it's much easier to use headphones. So, you have a situation when someone wants to share their music with their friends on the beach, at home, or the park. They may have concerns about how long the speakers' batteries will last, how big the speakers are, or if they are splash-proof.

You may write several different versions of your copy, each addressing different locations or concern. For example, and depending on the available characters, you may write something like this:

"Listen to your music on a sunny beach! Enjoy the highest sound quality for hours with our portable, waterproof Bluetooth speakers."

The first sentence tells a story. The second describes the product promoted in a way that answers your viewers' needs and concerns:

- "Highest sound quality" means that you don't get the tinny quality many associate with cheap speakers.
- "For hours" means long-lasting batteries.
- "Portable" means they are small and light.
- And "waterproof" means they are perfect for a beach, where they may get splashed with water.

By making every word count, we have only used 130 characters—well short of what Google requires (150-160 characters).

Maslow's hierarchy of needs

When thinking about people's needs, remember that our needs are not solely physical. Maslow's Hierarchy of Needs identifies five distinct levels:

- **Physiological needs**. These include everything we need to physically survive, e.g. air, water, food, shelter, sleep, clothing, and reproduction.

- **Safety needs.** These include personal security, employment, resources, health, and property.
- **Love and belonging.** These include needs such as friendship, intimacy, family, sense of connection.
- **Esteem.** Many Ads target these needs, which include respect, self-esteem, status, recognition, strength, and freedom.
- **Self-actualization.** This is the desire to become the most that one can be.

ANSWER TWO QUESTIONS

When writing Ad copy for a product or service, address two main questions that will arise in the viewer's mind:

- **How much does it cost?**
- **How hassle-free will it be to get it?**

You can pre-empt these common hurdles with some smart copy. For example, start by including the price, when possible. This not only addresses the first question, it also makes you look transparent.

In our example above, write:

"Listen to your music on a sunny beach! Enjoy the highest sound quality for hours with our portable, waterproof Bluetooth speakers, now available from $49."

The second question can also be easy to address:

"Listen to your music on a sunny beach! Enjoy the highest sound quality for hours with our portable, waterproof Bluetooth speakers, now available from $49. Free same-day delivery. Order now online!"

CALL TO ACTION (CTA)

You will notice above the addition of "Order now online!" This CTA (Call to Action) serves two purposes:

- One, it shows that ordering is fast and easy since you can do it online. This reassures the viewer that it is hassle-free.
- Two, it concludes the Ad copy by urging the reader to take action and place an order.

CTAs are among the most popular advertising tricks and I've devoted a full chapter to them. We'll get to that later. For now, all you need to remember is that it is good to end your Ad copy with a CTA.

OTHER KEY QUESTIONS

The examples used above assume that you are somewhat limited in the number of words you may use. However, we often have the luxury of longer copy—for example, when writing a sponsored blog post. While we must still make every word count, we may now expand our copy by exploring eight key questions about your customers' lives **before and after** purchasing the promoted product or service:

- **Questions 1 & 2: What** do your prospective customers **have** before purchasing your product or service? What do they have **after** purchasing it?
- **Questions 3 & 4: How** do your customers **feel** before purchasing your product or service? How do they feel **afterward**?
- **Questions 5 & 6: What is an average day like** for your customers before purchasing your product or service? What is it like **afterward**?

- **Questions 7 & 8: What is your customers' status** before purchasing your product or service? What is their status **afterward?**

These questions are formulated in such a way that addresses all possible needs a person may have. To write the perfect long copy, use them with Maslow's Needs to identify which specific needs the advertised product or services meets.

LONG VS SHORT COPY

There may be cases when you have an even greater luxury: that of choosing between long and short copy. Which one is right for you depends largely on your goals and audience.

Use longer copy when...

- You are advertising a service.
- You are targeting an older audience.
- Your copy will be used with an image or video which doesn't elaborate on the product or service you're advertising. For example, if you are asked to write copy for a Facebook post and the accompanying image is a generic one which doesn't include the service advertised, it is best to write longer copy.

Use shorter copy when...

- You are advertising a product.
- You are targeting a younger audience.
- The image or video accompanying the copy elaborates on the product you're advertising.

Your choice will also be influenced by the platform that you're advertising on. For example, Facebook has some copy appear above the image on posts—the so-called **post text**. Analyses have shown that post text between 20 and 75 words generates the highest reach.

USING LISTICLES AND NUMBERS

So-called **listicles** are a common way of creating highly clickable Ad copy. Listicles are explored in detail in a previous chapter, but, as a reminder, they are usually made up of a simple structure:

Number + Noun + Personal Pronoun + Modal.

For example: "9 Reasons You Should Wake Up Earlier."

Listicles and numbers work well in Ad copy, as they often serve as CTAs (Calls to Action). The structure is designed to pique viewers' interest in a way that encourages them to click on the Ad.

Check out the free online Headline Analyzer (https://coschedule.com/headline-analyzer) to test different Ad copy. While this tool is designed for headlines, it works well with Ad copy, too.

INCLUDE EMOTIONAL TRIGGERS

The easiest way to encourage people to click on an Ad is by provoking an emotional response. This makes some marketers focus on negative emotions like anger or fear. Their Ad copy effectively says something along the lines of, "Thousands of people die each year because they don't use our products. You're next!"

This kind of Ad copy is very effective in the short-term, as negative emotions are more powerful than positive ones. Indeed, studies show that we're hardwired to notice negative emotions first. That is why you may not remember the ten people who praised your work, but you will always remember the one who hated it.

However, **I never use negative emotions** in my Ad copy, as they create negative associations with the promoted product and company. Eventually, when people see the company's logo or Ads, they will experience physiological responses associated with fear, anger, and disgust. Once that happens, it is near impossible to overturn these, no matter how brilliant your future positive copy may be.

Instead of using negative emotions, use positive ones. **Affirmation** and **humour** are great ways to include a positive emotional trigger in your Ad copy.

AFFIRMATION

One way to trigger a positive emotional response is by appealing to people's innate sense of **entitlement**. Deep down, we all feel we deserve the best. Create great Ad copy by appealing to that feeling.

For example, an Ad with a headline, "#1 Divorce Lawyer in London—Protect Your Best Interest" uses that instinct perfectly. It also starts with a number for maximum impact.

As marketers know, most people tend to be self-centred. So, don't make the Ad about your client's awesome product, service, or—even worse—company. Quite frankly, no-one cares. However, everyone will pay attention if you show them how your product or service can make their lives easier. After all, they deserve the best!

HUMOUR

Studies suggest that humour affects positively viewers, attracts increased attention, and generates a positive attitude towards the product, service, or company.

Enhance its effect with careful consideration of the audience, situation, and type of humour.

Humour, however, is not advised when you wish to focus on the Ad's or company's credibility. Unsurprisingly, studies suggest that viewers don't take funny Ads seriously!

TERMS USED IN THIS CHAPTER

- **A/B Testing**: A process to perfect your Ads by constantly comparing them to each other and eliminating underperforming ones.

- **Ad copy**: the text included in your Ad.

- **CTA (Call To Action)**: A phrase or button, usually found at the end of your Ad copy, that explicitly asks the viewer to perform a specific action. For example, "Click here to find out more," "Buy now," "Learn more," "Contact us," etc.

- **Listicles**: An article that includes content in the form of a list. Ad copy that resembles listicle headlines can be very efficient in encouraging viewers to click on the Ad.

NOVICE MISTAKE TO AVOID

In writing Ad copy, there is no room for a "one size fits all" mentality. Every audience, product, service, and company is unique.

It may be tempting to develop a certain style and follow it with each client. However, you must set aside time for research and be prepared to follow a completely different approach with each new client.

INSIDER TIP

A crucial concept in marketing and advertising is that of **A/B testing**.

In A/B testing, you prepare several variations on an Ad, each with small changes to the rest. By running two of them simultaneously and keeping the more successful one, you will constantly be improving your Ads.

Ask your clients to perform A/B testing to perfect their Ads and find the best copy possible. This not only helps ensure the success of their advertising efforts, it also keeps you in touch with your client, shows your professionalism, and generates a steady source of income.

RAYNE'S SUGGESTION

People are so inundated with advertisements these days that most simply tune them out as unwanted distractions. As a copywriter, your main challenge is to win attention—and this has to be done in the fraction of a second before the viewer's eyes move past the Ad.

ASSIGNMENT

The goal of this exercise is to help you realise how different Ads must be, depending on the intended audience and platform used.

After studying the examples offered above, create Ad copy for two sets of Ads regarding "wireless speakers." Follow these guidelines:

- The first set of Ads will target home users who are 50-years-old and above.
- The second set will be addressed to young people using wireless speakers at the park.
- Each set will consist of three Ads.
- The first Ad will be up to 160 characters long. This is intended for use on Google.
- The second Ad will be between 50 and 100 words long. This is intended for use on Facebook.
- The third copy will be at least 300 words long. This is intended as a sponsored blog post. You may make it a listicle if you wish.

CHAPTER 11

MAKE THEM CLICK: THE CALL TO ACTION

Nicholas C Rossis

Calls to Action (CTAs) are the prompts you will often see at the end of a blog or social media post, directing you to your next step.

For example, "Buy Now!" is a CTA. So is "Click here to learn more about XYZ."

CTAs can take the form of a button or a link. They can be direct or subtle. Whatever the form, an effective CTA will draw your readers' attention, pique their interest, and lead them to the desired destination.

WHY USE A CTA?

CTAs are the darlings of marketers. This is because study after study proves their efficiency:

- Adding CTAs to your Facebook page can increase the click-through rate by 285%.

- Emails with a single call-to-action can increase clicks by up to 371% and sales by up to a whopping 1,617%.

- After Brafton added CTA buttons to article templates, they increased revenue by 83% in one month.

- HubSpot found that anchor text CTAs increased conversion rates by 121%.

- In blogs, 83% to 93% of each post's leads come from anchor text and internal link CTAs.

CTAs serve two main purposes:

- To **tell** someone what they should do.
- To give them the **motivation** to do so.

A successful CTA will address both of these.

ANALYSIS OF A LONG CTA

When I write long copy such as blog or social media posts, I end them with CTAs that have the following format:

How can we help? + Online contact + Phone + Happily ever after

For example:

- Are you looking for a new home? Contact us now online or call 12345 and find your dream house!

Let's analyse this structure.

HOW CAN WE HELP?

"How can we help?" is used to capture in a single sentence what my client does and how they can help readers. It can also be used to summarise what the blog post is about and remind people of the fun experiences they can have. For example, I might write a blog post promoting a hotel in Yucatan by describing the fun tourists can have diving in the ocean. In this case, I might end the post with a CTA like this:

- After a fun day diving in the crystal waters of Yucatan, relax with a cold drink in your hand in our hotel bar. Contact us now online or call 12345 and begin the vacation of a lifetime!

You will notice that I always strive to sell an experience; not a service.

ONLINE CONTACT

Online contact is a link to the online form where people can register, shop, book a room, learn more, etc. As soon as they finish reading our copy, we want them to click here.

CALL 12345

In many cases, we want people to **give our client a call**. Since many people will be reading our copy on their phones, adding a number makes it easier to do so: many phones automatically detect phone numbers and let readers dial with a simple tap (you can also add a simple code to turn numbers into a direct-dial link).

HAPPILY EVER AFTER

I use the "**happily ever after**" to remind people of the greater picture of how contacting my client will improve their life, offer them a unique experience, and generally make them happier. The difference with the "how can we help?" introduction is that the former refers to a specific experience, whereas the "happily ever after" refers to a generic one.

ANALYSIS OF A SHORT CTA

Unfortunately, we don't always have the luxury of a long CTA. Depending on the client and format, your CTA may be a simple prompt, e.g. "Shop now!" This is usually the case with **Ads** and **web copy** like a home page, where CTAs are in the form of buttons. Since buttons can't be too large, you must avoid long copy. In these cases, you have to use a different structure.

START WITH STRONG WORDS

In real life, we avoid strong words and action verbs because they come off as rude. Say you own a clothes shop. Following people around and barking "buy that dress now!" to your hapless customers may not be the best way to secure a sale.

With CTAs, it's the exact opposite. Instead of coming off as rude, you come off as direct. People unconsciously appreciate being directed in a clear way—and don't mind the strong verbs.

So, **start your CTA with a strong verb**: "Shop," "order," "buy," or "get" are perfectly acceptable.

Follow these with more powerful words; words that will elicit an emotional response from your audience or trigger their curiosity. For example, "cringeworthy," "mistakes," "hilarious," etc.

End with an **exclamation mark**. With my copy, I rarely use exclamation marks. CTAs, however, are much more powerful with one.

CREATE A REASON TO TAKE ACTION

Remember a CTA's twin purpose? On the one hand, it must tell people what they should do. On the other, it must motivate them to do so.

So, give them an incentive that motivates them. Tell them right away **how** they will benefit from doing what you ask them to. Will they save money? Lose weight and get fit? Grow hair in the right places instead of the wrong ones?

Fear of missing out (FOMO) is also a powerful incentive. Time-sensitive offers do much better because of this, as people fearing they might lose an opportunity are more likely to act.

"Shop today! Sale ends tomorrow," and "buy now while supplies last!" are great examples of using FOMO in your CTAs.

Whatever the motivation, make sure to stress it **using as few words as possible**. "Now 75% off" is much more effective than "order our fantastic product now, and we'll send you a coupon for 75% off."

USE NUMBERS

As with headlines, **numbers** in CTAs work wonders to increase conversion rates. Whenever you get the chance, use them to turn your average CTA into a great one. Even something as simple as "open 24/7" or "#1 restaurant in town" can encourage more people to click.

GET CREATIVE

With everyone using CTAs, it can be hard to be original. Even so, you have to try. For example:

- Instead of "Check out today's deals!" use "Tons of deals at your fingertips!"

- Instead of "Fill out the form to get started" use "A healthier life starts now!"

- Instead of "Call today for more information" use "Don't miss out! We're just a phone call away."

- Instead of "Buy now our fertiliser" use "Your yard sucks! Let us fix it" (yes, even crappy language has a place in CTAs).

TEST YOUR CTA

Congratulations, you have finally written your CTAs. Whether long or short, you should now test them.

I explain in the chapter "Writing Ad Copy" the concept and value of A/B testing, where you prepare several variations of your copy and run them simultaneously, keeping the more successful ones.

The same is true of CTAs. A small change in your call to action can make a big difference. You might not expect higher click-through rates as a result of changing a word or two but it happens all the time. This is why testing is so important.

Only test one thing at a time or it will be difficult to discern which change makes a difference. For example, test a newsletter CTA by sending one group of subscribers an email with "Shop Now!" as your CTA. Send the second group an email with "Shop Now Our Spring Collection" as the CTA. Don't change anything else, including the CTA's colour or placement.

EXAMPLES OF SHORT CTAS

The examples below are picked from Sumo (https://sumo.com/stories/power-words). Visit their website for more examples.

CTAs that encourage a purchase

- Shop now
- Shop now. Get 50% off.
- Act now
- Save today
- Buy now. Pay later.
- Yes! I want one.
- Order now
- Claim your coupon
- Start saving today
- Free gift with purchase

CTAs for content

- Learn more
- Curious? Read on
- Download now

- Keep reading
- Read the full story

CTAs for events

- Reserve your seat
- Register now
- Book your tickets
- Count me in!
- Sign me up
- Save me a spot

CTAs for service-based businesses

- Book your next appointment
- Start your free trial
- Yes! I want a free upgrade.
- Sign up and save

CTAs that focus on results

- See how your business benefits
- Start now. Get results.
- I'm ready to see a change

CTAs to collect feedback

- Complete our 5-minute survey
- Take a survey

- Leave a review
- Give us your feedback
- Let us know how we did

CTAs for social media

- Follow us
- Stay connected on social
- Like us on Facebook

NOVICE MISTAKES TO AVOID

When I first started writing web copy for home pages, I tended to write long CTAs. The developer finally snapped at me that I had to limit my CTAs to a maximum of three words, as they were to be used in the form of a button—and buttons must be short.

I now limit myself to the simplest of CTAs in my web copy.

INSIDER TIPS

With CTAs, small things can make a big change. **Use initial-caps** to increase clicks, as studies suggest that "Click Now For Our Spring Collection" works better than "Click now for our spring collection."

Also, suggest to your client that they test different **colours** to create striking CTAs. Mention that SAP found that orange CTAs boosted their conversion rate by 32.5%, while Performable found that red CTAs boosted their conversion rate by 21%. Your client will be impressed by your ability to offer ideas beyond the narrow scope of text!

RAYNE'S SUGGESTION

Be careful not to get pushy. Of course, this depends on the target audience, but most people are put off by a CTA like "Don't hesitate! Hurry!! Buy now!!!"

I prefer subtler CTAs which empower the target audience while moving towards the purchase: "Click here to find out more."

When I write Ad copy for my clients—most of whom are book authors and publishers—I use the CTA to invite people to download the free sample. It may be as brief as "Download a free sample" or use a longer version such as, "See for yourself if this book is right for you. Click here to download the first chapters free." Rather than getting pushed into a rushed purchase, readers feel respected and empowered to make a choice based on their personal taste.

ASSIGNMENT

Write three short CTAs for each of the categories mentioned above:

- CTAs that encourage a purchase
- CTAs for content
- CTAs for events
- CTAs for service-based businesses
- CTAs that focus on results
- CTAs to collect feedback
- CTAs for social media

CHAPTER 12

FROM ATTENTION TO ACTION: ADAPTING THE AIDA FORMULA

Rayne Hall

AIDA stands for **'Attention—Interest—Desire—Action.'** This formula has been used in advertising and promotion for over a hundred years. It's a great model for copywriting, especially Ad copy, sales emails and product descriptions.

Good copy arouses all four factors in the reader's mind—and they have to unfold in precisely this order, or they won't work.

ATTENTION

First, you need to get the potential buyers' attention. If they don't notice the advertisement or email, then it doesn't matter how beautifully crafted your copy is, because it won't get read.

Nowadays, this first step is the most challenging. People are so inundated with promotional messages that they've programmed their mind to simply tune them out. They may see hundreds or even thousands of advertisements and promotions every day and don't take the slightest bit of notice.

Your job as a copywriter is to get their attention—and this has to happen very fast. You have only a fraction of a second, or their glance will already have passed over the advert or scrolled past the email header.

Certain words can help capture the attention:

- Now
- Secrets
- Free
- How
- You
- Embarrass
- Shortcuts
- Introducing
- Revealed
- Only

However, take this list—and any other list of attention-grabbing power words—with a pinch of salt. What arrests the attention of one person causes another to pass by. This depends entirely on your client's target audience. For example, the word 'free' is a magnet for bargain hunters, but leaves others unmoved.

In my field, promoting books, certain words arouse the interest of certain readers. 'Rogue, governess, marriage of convenience, coming-out season, chaperone' thrill fans of Regency Romance novels, but have no effect whatsoever on Western readers who are more likely to respond to 'Sheriff, stagecoach, bank, posse, lynch, cowboy, ranch, outlaw.' I use the thrill words of the genre in subtitles and book blurbs.

Visuals can help greatly in getting instant attention. If it's part of your role, select eye-catching images for adverts, or work with the client's artists and designers.

INTEREST

Once the viewer has noticed the email header, advert or product picture, you need to tickle her curiosity, or she won't stop. You want her to click to open that email or read the product description.

Again, you need to use words that have an instant appeal to the target audience. Sometimes, the thrill words you've used to arrest the viewer's attention will serve to arouse her interest. (Although 'Attention' and 'Interest' are distinct stages, you can sometimes achieve them both with a single sentence.)

A neat trick for stimulating interest is to ask a question and plant it in the reader's mind. For example, the question 'What is the dark secret of the governess?' is likely to tickle Regency Romance readers.

DESIRE

Once you've grabbed the readers' attention and aroused their curiosity, the fun part comes. Here you can really use your copywriting skills. Make the readers want the service or item.

You achieve this by showing the benefits they can get.

Two useful techniques to try:

1. Create a sensory experience in their mind (e.g. by describing sounds, scents, the sensation of touch)
2. Evoke their emotions.

ACTION

Now that the readers want the item, motivate them to do something about it right away, otherwise the effect is lost.

Most often, the action you want them to take is to click: Ask them to click to subscribe to a newsletter, sign a petition, ask for a quote, get a free e-book, listen to a music sample, add an item to a favourites list, or put a product into their virtual shopping basket.

In the previous chapter 'Calls to Action,' Nicholas has shown you how to achieve this crucial step.

NOVICE MISTAKE TO AVOID

Don't take it for granted that the viewer will notice the email, advertisement, or product listing. You have to get their attention, and you have to get it instantly, or the message will get lost in a sea of other promotions.

INSIDER TIP

Where possible, appeal to the senses or emotions of the target audience, especially in the Desire section. For this, you need to understand how these people feel.

NICHOLAS' SUGGESTION

A great way to test AIDA is to run a series of A/B tests. These are explained in detail in later chapters but the basic idea is to run two sets of AIDA Ads and see which one performs better. Keep that and discard the other. Then, design a new Ad and test it against the one you've kept. By repeating this process, you will end up with killer Ads!

ASSIGNMENTS

1. Study an advertisement, sales email or other promotional text for which you are the target audience. (For example, if you love pizza, study how a pizza delivery company coaxes you into ordering.) What does the company do to win your Attention, Interest, Desire, Action? See if you can break the copy down into those components.

2. Think about your client's target audience. Which words are likely to grab their attention and/or arouse their curiosity? Compile at least five words. You can use them in the future for the Attention and Interest phases.

CHAPTER 13

THE TRICKIEST ASSIGNMENT: CRAFTING SALES EMAILS

Rayne Hall

In the early days of the Internet, sales emails replaced sales letters, and they played a huge role in marketing. Their impact is shrinking now, especially for mass mailings that get automatically consigned to spam folders. However, in some situations, sales emails are still required and have an impact.

I write a specific kind of sales email for a specific kind of client: query letters from authors to agents and publishers. The recipients say on their websites what kind of books they're interested in, and invite authors to contact them. I then write query letters (sales emails) which provide the precise information the publishers want, presented in the format and style that captures the recipient's attention.

Other industries also have situations where sales emails are customary and welcome, and you'll be called upon to write them.

The most likely kind of sales letter you will get hired to write is a reply to an enquiry. When customers contact your client with a website comment to request information about the product, a well-crafted reply can lead to a sale. Make it **as personal as possible** and address the enquirer by name.

The client may then want to send a **follow-up email** to those enquirers who haven't responded. This needs to be phrased carefully, to avoid annoying the recipients. Basically, the follow up email should be casual, helpful and brief. "Hi [name], I'm wondering if you've received my answer of [date]. Do you have further questions, anything I can help you with? Joe."

I don't recommend more than one follow-up. Anyone who still hasn't responded is not interested, and there's no point pestering them. Some clients persist in firing off email after email to anyone who ever enquired. Those emails simply land in spam folders, and harm the sender's standing with mail service providers.

Haranguing people with continued emails can also be illegal. Laws are constantly evolving to protect users from spam and abuse. The most important rule to be aware of is the **General Data Protection Regulation (GDPR)** of the European Union. If someone lives in a European Union country, it's illegal to even store their data and email address without their consent. (That's why most companies move away from follow-up sales emails and shift towards newsletters. Once a prospect has subscribed, you may contact them regularly.)

THE BIG CHALLENGE: GETTING THE EMAIL OPENED

If an email looks like marketing message, most people don't bother to open it. With dozens of emails arriving in their inbox, they won't even glance at the subject header unless it jumps out at them.

So the trickiest part is crafting a subject line that draws attention and whets enough interest for recipients to open the email. (These are the first two steps of the AIDA formula.)

Use thrill words that you know the target audience will respond to, for example the ones you compiled for the assignment in the AIDA chapter.

However, stay clear of words that trigger mail servers' spam alerts. If the subject line contains words like *free, discount, special offer, buy*, the email may automatically get redirected into spam folders.

A strategy that worked well for a while was to incorporate the recipient's name in the subject line. "Christine, here's your information." However, overuse has diminished the impact of this approach.

NOVICE MISTAKE TO AVOID

Don't write overt, pushy sales messages which get intercepted by spam filters and never reach the recipient.

INSIDER TIP

Personalisation is everything. Even if you have to send the same information to 100 people, phrase it so that each of them feels that it's personal. Use the word 'you' several times, especially in the first paragraph.

NICHOLAS' SUGGESTION

I get requests every day from people who wish to publish a guest post on my author blog (nicholasrossis.me). I can always tell who's going to send me a well written post from the query email.

My blog is aimed at a very specific kind of people: writers and authors. From my experience, we writers love books, reading, and history. We also have to learn about book marketing. So, the vast majority of my posts cover these topics.

My main request from anyone wishing to publish a post on my blog is that the topics they suggest are of interest to my visitors. I make that very clear on my contact page and have an extensive FAQ dedicated to that.

Every day I marvel at how few people actually send me a generic email along the lines of "I love your blog and would like to write for you. I promise my post will be unique and well written. Looking forward to hearing from you." Only too often, the email has typos and grammar mistakes. And sometimes I get suggested topics that have absolutely nothing to do with my audience (no, my writer friends don't care about bitcoins).

So, please take the time necessary to tailor your email to the intended recipient or your email risks getting ignored.

ASSIGNMENT

Look through your email spam folder. What kind of emails got caught there? Identify what words and phrases may have triggered the spam filter, so you can avoid them in the sales emails you write.

CHAPTER 14

MORE THAN FACTS: HOW TO CREATE ENTICING PRODUCT DESCRIPTIONS

Rayne Hall

Product descriptions are printed on packaging and in catalogues. These days, most are in online catalogues, either on the client's own website or on a retail website.

GET THE TONE AND CONTENT RIGHT

Know who the readers are:

- If they are **businesses** (e.g. wholesalers, tradesmen), the description should be factual and to the point, emphasising features and using industry jargon.

- If they are **end consumers** (e.g. restaurant visitors, holiday makers, supermarket shoppers), the copy should emphasise benefits. The writing style can be more creative, appealing to emotions and senses.

You should also know whether the target audience are **experienced users** or **first-time buyers.** This will tell you whether or not to include basic information. What a beginner finds helpful can feel patronising to an advanced user.

What do they want to know? Some customers are interested in the name of the garment's designer, for what occasions it can be worn, and what are the best ideas for accessorising. Others care about in which country it was manufactured, if the employment conditions in the factory meet 'fair trade' standards, and if the dyes used are synthetic or natural. Yet others want to know what percentage of wool the fabric contains and if the garment can be machine-washed. Your product description should answer the questions the target audience wants to know.

SHORT AND LONG FORMS

Short descriptions: Some catalogues allow only two or three lines of description. Keep the copy succinct, and focus on how the product differs from the others on that page. You may want to use a tagline. (See the chapter on Taglines and Slogans.)

Long descriptions: Follow the AIDA formula, aim to evoke senses, and arouse emotions. You may want to present some of the information with bullet points.

Sometimes, viewers can click on the short product description to see the longer one. In this case, you need to write two versions. The short form serves for the Attention and Interest steps of AIDA, while the long version creates the Desire and triggers the Action.

MY PERSONAL SPECIALISM

I write a lot of product descriptions—and since I specialise in working for authors and publishers, these are usually **book blurbs and synopses.**

The difference lies in the target audience. A book blurb is intended for book readers, including fans of that genre. It gets published on bookselling sites like Barnes & Noble and Amazon, and also on the back cover of paperbacks. It tells the reader what the book is about without giving away the full plot, arouses emotions including curiosity, and serves to whet the reader's appetite. It entices readers to download the free sample and ultimately buy the book.

A synopsis, on the other hand, is a structured plot summary intended for industry experts (publishers, literary agents, acquisition editors). In a few paragraphs, it demonstrates how the author has handled the plot and enables them to judge whether the book is right for their programme.

You may wonder why authors need a copywriter to craft their blurbs and synopses. Many authors feel inhibited when it comes to describing their own books. They struggle to extract the bare bones and to present the plot in the kind of synopsis that publishing professionals want to see. Some authors get cold sweat and stomach cramps when they try. Others can't write the emotionally enticing, curiosity-arousing blurb needed to tempt readers.

I've built a reputation as an expert who knows how to craft powerful blurbs and synopsis. One day you may be known as the go-to writer for product descriptions in your niche—whether that is furniture or financial services, sports gear or computer apps.

CREATING DESCRIPTIONS BASED ON PICTURES ALONE

Sometimes, a client will provide you with a photo of the product and request you to write a description from the picture alone. If this is the same photo that will be published, you will see only what the target audience can see for themselves, which makes the description in part futile.

In this case, focus on evoking senses and emotions. However, I urge you to obtain factual information about the product and not just to indulge in lyrical creativity.

A LESSON LEARNT FROM MY EARLY EXPERIENCE

Early in my writing career, part of my job was to craft descriptions for women's apparel. I received a lot of praise for my creative approaches, so I thought I was really good. But… I assumed things without checking my assumptions.

Typically, I received photos of the dresses from the new collections as soon as they were photographed, and it was my job to write descriptions which would then get published in glossy women's magazines.

One photo showed a seated model wearing a lovely turquoise-coloured dress, displaying her slender legs. All the other gowns were long, so this one really stood out. I described it as a 'mini dress' and waxed lyrical about wearing short gowns at formal functions.

A few days later—after the magazine was printed—I attended a trade fair and saw the actual dress. I gasped, and felt the blood drain from my face. The dress was a long one! The skirt had slits from hem to hip, and when the model posed seated, the legs showed while the fabric faded into the background. I wonder how many customers bought this garment expecting it to be a 'mini' dress.

After this embarrassment I always asked for factual information from the client or the manufacturer, and I insisted on seeing all the photos from the photo shoot (showing the dress from different angles), not just the one selected for publication.

NOVICE MISTAKES TO AVOID

Don't overload your product descriptions with adjectives. (Romantic, stunning, purple, short...) Adjectives are useful in descriptions, but if you cluster too many of them together, the copy feels clunky and forced.

Beware hyperbole. Some new writers exaggerate the product's benefits, and the result is ridiculous and undermines the target audience's trust. I remember some years ago I wanted to buy a detangling hair brush, and found one in a local shop. I read the product description on the cardboard packaging: it promised that this was a 'life-changing brush.' I didn't buy.

NICHOLAS' SUGGESTION

Different products have wildly different requirements. For example, I have written extensively for cannabinoids (CBD, THC, etc.). The legal situation is such that I have to walk a fine line between describing their health potential while avoiding making any medical claims—or the client faces significant fees from the authorities.

It's not as simple as adding a disclaimer at the end of the article. Every word that I write is chosen in a way that corresponds to that basic need. For example, I would never say that "CBD can alleviate pain." Instead, I'd say, "Studies suggest that CBD may alleviate pain." The first is an unproven medical claim; the second is a fact.

When describing a product make sure that you understand the specifics of that product and industry before you start writing!

ASSIGNMENT

For this exercise, I want you to pick a product you've used today—perhaps the cereal you had for breakfast, the slippers you're wearing, the e-reader you hold in your hand now—and write a product description of 150-200 words. Write it so that it appeals to a target audience, and assume that the target audience consists of people like you.

CHAPTER 15

THE IDEAL GIG FOR FICTION WRITERS: BRAND STORY TELLING

Rayne Hall

Brand storytelling is a relatively new form of promotional text. In the past, businesses would publish boring 'company histories' comprising of dull dates and facts.

Now they seek to **tell a story that fascinates readers**. This is where **experienced fiction writers excel:** you know how to hook readers, present characters, construct a plot, and arouse emotions. Tell the story of the brand as if it was a novel—only, of course, much shorter.

FOCUS ON CHARACTERS

Just as in a work of fiction, it's the characters that the reader cares about. Who's the main character? Most likely, this is the company's founder. Put her at the centre of your story. (If the brand has existed for generations and changed hands, still focus on the founder, but you may have to switch to other characters later.)

THE START-UP SCENARIO

Currently, there's great interest in start-ups. Where did the idea come from? How did the founder identify the niche? What problem existed that he tried to solve with his new product? How did the company operate at the start, before it became profitable? Where did the founder get the courage and stamina to pursue her vision?

READERS LOVE UNDERDOGS

In brand stories, just like in novels, readers root for the underdog—the person who faces injustice, prejudice, discrimination, cruelty, or seemingly insurmountable obstacles, but perseveres. In what way was the founder an 'underdog'? Perhaps he was shunned in his community because of his gender orientation, looked down upon because of his skin colour, mocked for his stutter, distrusted because of his family's criminal history? Maybe his parents were so poor that he couldn't go to college, or they had to flee their home war-torn home country and he had no chance to go to school. Use this, and show how he succeeded despite all.

EMPHASISE THE MISSION

What's the brand's mission—other than making money for its owners and investors? Find the 'socially responsible' element. Does this brand want to provide low-cost quality footwear that poor people can afford, or environmentally-responsible holiday trips which protect the nature? Ideally, find a link between this social mission and the founder's start-up vision.

CONNECT THE PRESENT TO THE BEGINNING

In the last sentence or paragraph, show how the brand honours the founder's vision. "And today, we still build AABB, the way XX YY did in his garage."

NOVICE MISTAKES TO AVOID

Don't try to tell the whole history of the brand. Just focus on the details that will capture the readers' imagination.

PROFESSIONAL TIP

Let the brand's archetype inspire the story you write, both in content and word choice (see the chapter on Archetypes.)

NICHOLAS' SUGGESTION

Study the company to make sure that everything you write is in harmony with the brand they are projecting. If the company is portraying itself as cool and sophisticated, writing an imaginary story about how scruffy the founder was as a young student working in his garage may well clash with this image and cost you the job.

ASSIGNMENT

Find the brand stories of several leading brands, and study them. Can you find the elements I've described, for example, main character at the centre of the story, the 'underdog' succeeding against the odds, the social mission?

OPTIONAL

If you have a client—whether it's a paying client or a friend whom you're trying to help with her start-up—work with them to create a brand story. Do you have fiction writing experience? Then use your storytelling skills, because they give you an advantage over other copywriters.

CHAPTER 16

WHAT KIND OF PERSON IS THIS? CRAFTING THE CLIENT'S BIO

Rayne Hall

Many clients want you to write bios for them—for example, for their social media accounts, websites, and product sleeves.

If the client is an individual, such as a musician, author, artist, politician, social media influencer, or spiritual leader, focus on the archetype he represents, let his **personality** shine through, and make him appear human and authentic.

If the client is a corporation or business, you may be requested to write bios for all team members, or for all executive staff, to display on a website. There may be little room for showing personality. Communicate with each person for whom you write the bio to get the facts right and ensure they're happy with what you say about them. However, some executives may only spare you a couple of minutes, so don't waste their time.

The bio is like a business card. It shows new acquaintances who this person is, so they can decide whether this is someone with whom they want to connect.

It needs to be right not just for the individual it portrays, but for the company he or she represents, and for the place where it gets published. Try to incorporate phrases that evoke his archetype, use a tone that suits the publication, and choose content that arouses the readers' interest.

You may write more than one bio for your client, with different lengths and varying content. Perhaps you'll create a super-short one for Twitter and a longer one for a website, a factual one for the company's 'who is who' directory, and a quirky one for guest blog posts.

WHAT TO INCLUDE

State the client's **role**—this could be his job title, position in the organisation, or the activities he carries out.

Sometimes, a list of roles works well: 'virtual assistant, translator, trouble-shooter' or 'landscape designer, gardener, handyman.' Don't use more than three, because this can appear unfocused.

Try to include **a personal touch,** because most people crave connecting with a real person—but be careful not to reveal more than the client is comfortable with, or what is appropriate for the publication.

Good 'personal touch' details are:

- hobbies
- where he lives (the country, the town, the type of building or landscape)
- marital or family status (basics only)
- pets

Choose the kind of detail that appeals to the readers of that publication. Is your client guest posting on a DIY blog? Mention that he lives in a converted barn and enjoys restoring furniture. Is he getting featured on his city's website? State the town quarter where he resides, how long he's lived there, what he loves about the city and which local sports team he supports. Is this bio for the company website? Include his specialisms, skills, and qualifications.

Important: a bio is not a CV/resume! You don't have to give a complete history of the client's life. Choose a few important and interesting aspects and leave out the rest.

NOVICE MISTAKES TO AVOID

To protect the family's privacy and safety, don't reveal the names and ages of spouses and children. 'Mother of three, grandmother of five' or 'lives with his wife and two children in...' is enough.

PROFESSIONAL TIP

Write a 'flexible' bio—one that can be adjusted for several purposes. Structure it so that certain paragraphs can be included or left out, depending on the purpose and required length.

NICHOLAS' SUGGESTION

When someone has had a rich professional career, it can be hard to choose which aspects to emphasise. You have two options here. The first one is to pick those which most match the company. For example, if you are writing a company website bio for the founder of an investment company who used to be a musician before, you may focus on his financial career rather than his musical one.

The second is to write a "modular" bio. As Rayne suggests above, structure it in a way that lets the company easily remove any paragraphs they don't need, depending on the medium on which the bio will be published. That way, your bio can still be used on both a Rolling Stone's story on musicians who pursued a different career and a WSJ feature story of successful investors. The company simply needs to remove any elements that don't match the medium in question.

Copywriting

ASSIGNMENT

Write two versions of a bio for someone—either for a client or for yourself. Make the first one short (circa 100 words) and the second one longer (300 words).

CHAPTER 17

INTERVIEWING YOUR CLIENT: PICK THE RIGHT QUESTIONS, CHOOSE THE BEST ANSWERS

Rayne Hall

When your client gets interviewed for a magazine, blog, podcast, or other medium, he'll need your guidance on what to say and how to say it.

Most interviews these days are pre-written rather than live. The publication sends the questions and the interviewee has time to think out the answers and edit them.

Work with your client to craft the best answers. The client's first idea may not be the best, and you'll need to **draw out alternative answers until you hit gold**. Then you phrase the answers so they sound vivid and entertaining.

RECURRING QUESTIONS

You'll soon observe which questions your client gets asked again and again in interviews. Once you've chosen the best answer, you can use it repeatedly. Simply phrase it in slightly different words.

Typical questions:

How did you get into this?

When did you start....?

Where do you get your ideas from?

What's your favourite...., and why?

Don't give the same answers that the competitors give to recurring questions. Almost every pianist says that he's been playing the piano from a young age, almost every artist that she's passionate about painting. **Get your client to say something different.**

"TELL US SOMETHING SURPRISING ABOUT YOURSELF"

This question comes up a lot. It's a lazy question: the interviewer wants to get an interesting answer, without going to the trouble of finding an interesting question first.

This is not the time to expose skeletons in the client's cupboard, or to reveal that she has six toes on her left foot. Instead, probe for **a factoid that's relevant to the product or brand.**

What experience in **the client's childhood or youth** could link to the product he's promoting? You can use this to either tug at the reader's emotions, or to make them chuckle.

Here are two sample replies, one stirring emotions, the other entertaining:

"I'm adopted, and have never been able to find my birth mother, even though I tried. I often lie awake, wondering what she was like, what made her give up her baby, and where she is now. Once I thought I was close to finding her, through a lead in Missouri, but the lead fizzled out. The song, 'Unknown Missouri Lady' on my new album is inspired by that quest."

"When I was eight or nine years old and people asked me what I wanted to be when I grew up, I replied, 'pirate queen'. I visualised myself on board a ship, cutlass in hand, with a fetching red head scarf fluttering in the wind. I soon realised that this wasn't realistic, and chose a more realistic career in fashion design. But the old fantasy is still there.... and you can see elements of it in my current collection. The red headscarves, the leather bodices, the broad belts... they all hark back to my pirate fantasies."

STAY POSITIVE

Keep the tone of the interviews upbeat. Briefly acknowledge difficulties (don't deny them), but focus on the constructive action the client is taking to deal with them.

DEALING WITH CONTROVERSIAL ISSUES

If the client is involved in any kind of controversy, interviewers will bring up the subject. The best way to handle this is to acknowledge the issue, state that the client is actively working on a constructive solution, and leave it at that.

"Yes, there's been an arson attack on our factory and the fire alarm system was sabotaged. Two of our workers suffered severe burns. Our thoughts are with injured women and their families. We are working with the police to investigate what happened. We have installed a new alarm system and fitted all the rooms with additional sprinklers."

Important: if the issue involves (or may lead to) any kind of legal dispute, it's important that you consult with the client's lawyers before releasing interview answers. They may advise you not to answer a particular question, or to phrase the reply differently.

LIVE INTERVIEWS

Anticipate the most likely questions, and choose the answers the client will give. However, don't write the answers down, otherwise the client may memorise and recite them, which would make a bad impression.

NOVICE MISTAKES TO AVOID

Never lie in interviews, though you and your client may be selective about which truths to tell.

INSIDER TIP

If you expect a big surge of interest in your client (for example, if he's been nominated for a major award or is about to release a sensational new product), prepare as many interview answers as you can.

You can probably predict most of the questions. Agree with the client about what to say, then write the same thing in different ways, to insert in different interviews. This way, your client will have fewer interview questions to think about during a time when he's frantically busy.

NICHOLAS' SUGGESTION

It can be easy to get carried away with interviews, especially if your client hasn't given you much to go on. However, avoid letting your imagination get the best of you. For example, don't invent a clash between the founder and her overbearing father or distrusting bank manager, no matter how good that story would look in a novel or how these details would fit your narrative.

ASSIGNMENT

Make a list of at least five interview questions that you expect your client will be asked. (If you don't have a real client yet, do this for a friend.)

Obtain the answers, and paraphrase them in two different ways.

CHAPTER 18

ENTERTAINING THE CLIENT'S CUSTOMERS: NEWSLETTERS

Rayne Hall

Newsletters are gaining in importance, replacing sales emails more and more. By subscribing to a newsletter, potential customers consent to receive communications, and that's what companies want. Many businesses employ every available tool to get newsletter subscribers—pop-ups, incentives (free gifts), personalised advice.

Once they have the subscriber base, they need to produce the material to feed the newsletter, and that's often the copywriter's job. Therefore, newsletter-writing can be a growth market for you to tap into.

WHAT TO PUT IN THE NEWSLETTER

Don't just fill the newsletter with 'buy-buy-buy' messages, because those bore subscribers. You need to provide real content that the readers value.

Here are some ideas:

- **A news item.** What's new in your client's company? The launch of a new product or service? A new branch opening? Use this as the opener.

- **A special offer.** This should either be a subscriber-only discount, or the subscribers should be the first to know about it.

- **A contest or prize draw.** The rules must be clear, and include a closing date, who is eligible to enter, and the name of the contest judge who may not be part of the company. (Your client may not be aware what the rules are, or not realise that they must be published. It's your responsibility to obtain and convey this information.)

- If the client is an individual rather than a company, include **a personal titbit.**

- **A tip,** e.g. a short piece of professional advice from the client to the subscriber.

- **A joke,** perhaps a subject-related funny cartoon.

You don't need all of these. Choose what works best.

STYLE

Write in the **client's voice**. Use the style and words you've identified in the Archetypes chapter.

Write in the client is an individual rather than a company, write in the **first person** where possible.

Keep the style tight (no wordy waffling) and the paragraphs short.

Include invitations to communicate with the client. ("What do you think? I'd love to hear your opinion.")

Include clickable links to products, people and websites mentioned.

End with a friendly greeting and—if appropriate—the client's name.

NOVICE MISTAKE TO AVOID

Don't fill the newsletter with sales messages because nobody wants to read a lot of those. When faced with boring, blatant advertising, subscribers hit 'unsubscribe'.

INSIDER TIP

My favourite strategy for making a newsletter personal without infringing on the client's private life is to write about **the client's pet.** Subscribers love to read about sweet animals, and often look forward to the next instalment to find out more. Cute photos are a must.

NICHOLAS' SUGGESTION

First of all, I subscribe to dozens of newsletters. Rayne's is one of a handful I'm actually looking forward to. She shares funny titbits about everyday life in Bulgaria (who can forget her first-time experience of a Bulgarian feast); welcome tips, and makes it a point not to bore her reader with sales spiel. If you haven't subscribed to her newsletter yet, you should do so—and study each of her newsletters to learn how to perfect your art!

Many newsletters are never read. That's when a follow-up comes in handy. Technology here is your friend. Most email sending services (SendGrid, MailPoet, MailChimp, etc) let you segment your recipient lists. This way, you can target only specific segments instead of bothering everyone on your recipient list.

After sending your email, wait for a week, then resend it to those who haven't opened your email. You can repeat this process one more time, if you wish, but I'd suggest against doing it any more times.

When it comes to email lists, less is often more. You're much better off having 1,000 recipients and a 50% open rate (i.e. 500 people have opened your email) than 10,000 recipients and a 1% open rate (i.e. 100 people have opened it). Since most services charge you based on the number of recipients, it's much cheaper, too!

ASSIGNMENT

Make a list of specific items you could put into a client's newsletter. You can do this for one of your existing clients, or use a friend's project for this exercise.

CHAPTER 19

HOW TO HOOK FOLLOWERS WITH FUN AND TIPS: SOCIAL MEDIA POSTS

Rayne Hall

Social media are a growth sector for copywriters. More and more clients hire freelancers to produce posts for Facebook, Twitter, and other networks.

However, it's a rapidly changing field. Strategies which brought great results last year are now so over-used as to have little effect. You and your clients will need to adapt your approach continuously.

GUIDELINES

- **Mix up 'promotional' with 'non-promotional' posts.** Constant 'Buy, buy, buy!' messages don't hold the followers' interests.

- Keep social media posts short. **Bite-sized pieces get most attention.**

- Followers value 'tips' articles. What **practical advice and suggestions** can your client offer? Keep them relevant to the topic. For example, a fashion house may offer suggestions about how to accessorise, a cosmetics firm reveals how to ensure that lipstick stays on, a luggage manufacturer advises on how to pack a suitcase.

- **Aphorisms work superbly well**—but to come up with aphorisms related to your client's brand requires serious creativity. For example, if your client is a shoe brand, you would come up with thoughtful and funny one-liners about shoes, boots, walking, and feet.

- Promotional posts work best if you **focus on the product's benefits** (what the buyer will get out of it).

- **Product launches and special offers** get more attention than ordinary promotional posts.

- Humour gets attention. **Funny memes and cartoons** are great tools. You may need to use stock images or work with illustrators and designers for this.

- If your client is an individual (e.g. an actor or a scientist), create personal posts, giving **glimpses into the client's life.** This will require a delicate balance between preserving the client's privacy and the feeding the fans' curiosity. My favourite solution for this is to write about the client's pets. This has the additional advantage that you can use photos—and pictures of cute cats and dogs are the winners in the social media attention stakes.

- Write and upload a batch of social media posts and **schedule** them to go out at different times.

- Organise the social media posts into two groups: topical ones which will be shared only once (a report from the award ceremony, news that the dog is recovering well from the surgery) and **evergreen content** (e.g. cartoons, aphorisms) that can be used repeatedly, e.g. weekly or monthly.

- Some kinds of posts can be published across all social media, while others may need to be adapted to suit the medium.

NOVICE MISTAKES TO AVOID

Don't try to force attention by writing text IN CAPITAL LETTERS or by using a lot of exclamation marks!!!

INSIDER TIP

Have you written an instructional listicle-type blog post for client? You may be able to repurpose it by breaking it up into several bite-sized social media posts.

NICHOLAS' SUGGESTION

Rayne has written Twitter for Writers; an excellent book on using Twitter that I strongly advise you read. I don't really use Twitter half as much as I should, so I've followed her advice on my author blog and have gained tens of thousands of followers as a result. Even better, these are real people that I have real interactions with.

If I had to sum my social media policy, that would be, "be real, be fun, be helpful":

- **Be real**. Don't pretend you're happy if you've just lost a loved one. People know when you're faking it. You don't want to be labelled another fake influencer.

- **Be fun**. Even when you're down, try to smile. And do try to keep it positive. There are too many media outlets that focus on the negative and people desperately need a ray of sunshine. Be that and they'll come back on a daily basis.

- **Be helpful**. Help people asking you for advice. I happen to believe in Karma but this is not just about being kind; it can also be hugely beneficial. I once answered a dear old lady's question on self-publishing on LinkedIn and next thing I knew she had given me a year's worth of work. As she put it, "no one else had bothered to respond."

ASSIGNMENT

This is a challenging exercise, but worth doing, because it will really hone your copywriting skills. Try to come up with aphorisms (witty sayings) for your client's social media account.

Copywriting

Do this exercise even if the client hasn't asked you for social media posts. If you don't have a client yet, do it for an imaginary client, i.e. a friend's start-up business or a charity you support. The purpose is to train your mind to come up with ideas.

Start by making word lists. Write down all words that relate to the client's product, service or brand. For example, for a bed-manufacturing business, include bed, sleep, mattress, bedroom, nap, doze, snore... Allow your imagination to take leaps. When I think 'bed' and 'nap' I see a cat napping on the bed—so 'cat' goes on the list, too.

Then try to connect some of these words in funny and thoughtful ways. At first, ideas may be slow to arrive, but once you get started, they'll suddenly arrive while you take a shower or wash the dishes. Write down all your ideas, even the ones that don't strike you as great. After a few days, evaluate them and choose the best.

CHAPTER 20

AWAKEN THE POET WITHIN: COMPOSING TAGLINES AND SLOGANS

Rayne Hall

Condensing a brand into a single line—or even just a few words—is the highest, most difficult form of copywriting. You won't be asked to do this often, because most clients need a slogan only once and then stick with it forever. But if you crack this skill, you can market yourself as a slogan-writing specialist and potentially command high fees.

WHAT'S THE DIFFERENCE?

The definitions overlap. Taglines are sometimes called slogans, and slogans taglines. Sometimes, a one-liner serves both purposes. So, don't sweat the definitions, as long as you understand what your client is after.

Here are the broad definitions:

Taglines are very short, memorable summaries of what the brand stands for. Typically, they consist of just one sentence, or sometimes two very short sentences. They convey what the product or service is about, and focus on benefits:

- "When you care enough to send the very best" (Hallmark)
- "Antibacterial Protection for a Healthier Mouth" (Colgate)
- "PayPal is New Money" (PayPal)

Copywriting

Slogans are even shorter, just a few words. They rarely say what a product or service is about. Instead, they focus on the underlying attitude:

- "Just do it." (Nike)
- "Because you're worth it" (L'Oreal)
- "All for Freedom. Freedom for All." (Harley Davidson)

HOW TO CRAFT SLOGANS AND TAGLINES

Make three lists of words: one for the product's benefits, one for the archetype's words, and one related to the brand's image and attitude.

Many writers find it helps to create a 'word basket'. For this, find a pretty basket or other container. Then write the words on coloured paper or cardboard, cut them out, place them into the basket and shake them up. Now treat it as a creative game. Pick two or three words at random from the basket, and create a sentence with them.

Write down anything that sounds even halfway good.

Let a day pass, then read those sentences. Pick the ones you feel have potential, and refine and tighten them.

Speak them out loud and listen to the rhythm, because rhythm can make slogans sing.

ARE YOU A POET?

As an experienced writer of poems or lyrics, you already possess valuable skills for slogan writing. Your brain is accustomed to finding the right words and arranging them in the right order to achieve the best rhythm and sound. Use this to your advantage.

NOVICE MISTAKE TO AVOID

Don't try to cram a lot of information into a tagline. Less is best.

INSIDER TIPS

Try using alliteration (several words starting with the same sound).

Examples:

"Don't dream it. Drive it." (Jaguar)

"Intel Inside." (Intel)

"The best four by four by far."(Land Rover)

You can also use euphonics. Certain sounds have certain effects on the reader's and listener's subconscious. For example, the letter 'P' conveys authority while 'M' suggests comfort.

NICHOLAS' SUGGESTION

Slogans and taglines are all about creativity. Use any creativity exercise you know, from free association (saying the first word that comes to mind) to eating salmon (whose Omega fatty acids stimulate brain function) and taking long walks.

Personally, I'm at my most creative just before I fall asleep or when I've just woken up and I'm in that hazy state between sleep and wakefulness. One trick used by some writers is to doze off sitting on a chair with a pencil in your hand while thinking of the problem at hand. When you start drifting to sleep, the pencil will drop and wake you up. Write down any ideas that have come to you in that state.

ASSIGNMENT

Slogan-writing is an advanced-level skill. Develop your ability through practice before you attempt to write slogans for a real client.

Pick an object that's currently on your left (for me, this would be my tall coffee mug, a pair of scissors, the internet router or the wood stove.) Compile a word basket, focusing on the object's function and benefits, as well as anything else that comes to your mind. Now play the game, drawing two or three words at a time, and combining them into sentences.

The more often you practice this, the better you'll get.

CHAPTER 21

GETTING RANKED: HOW SEARCH ENGINES WORK

Nicholas C Rossis

Every time you run an online search, you get a Search Engine Results Page (**SERP**) that includes two kinds of results: **Ads** and so-called **organic results**.

This is not only true for search engines like Google. For an example, search for a product on Amazon. Notice how the entire top row of the results' page consists of Ads, whereas the results below that are organic.

Social media, too, acts like search engines. They select specific Ads to show you based on your past searches and interests. When Facebook, for example, displays Ads as part of your timeline, it does so according to what it knows about you. The rest of the material shown on your timeline, however, is chosen organically.

But how exactly is this content chosen?

Amazon, Google, Facebook... No matter the platform, all search engines work the same way: they use different criteria when choosing an Ad and when choosing organic content.

In the case of Ads, search engines use the **so-called auction model**.

THE AUCTION MODEL

Gone are the days when you chose an Ad to appear on your website and that was it. Nowadays, every time you run a search, you trigger a bidding war behind the scenes that concludes in milliseconds. With dozens, if not hundreds, of Ads competing against each other for the right to appear on your screen, search engines have to be pretty smart when selecting the best ones for you.

They do so by making the Ads compete against each other in a lightning-fast auction. The Ads are chosen based on several criteria, including how relevant they are to you personally and how high a bid, the marketer who made the Ad, is willing to make.

ORGANIC SEARCHES

Organic results are similar to the auction model—only, no bidding takes place. Just like with Ads, search engines of any kind wish to display the most relevant organic results to you. This triggers a competition that's every bit as fierce as that for Ads—indeed, even more so.

The website that appears at the very top of Google's SERP gets one-third of all clicks. Conversely, under 1% of people click on anything from the second page.

To choose the websites that appear on the coveted first page, search engines use a **ranking** system. Websites that rank highly have more chances of appearing first.

RANKING

Accurately ranking a website (or product, if you're searching on Amazon) matters hugely to search engines. **Not every search engine makes its money the same way.** Whereas Google cares about how long you spend on a website you visit after clicking on an Ad; they don't care if you actually buy something or not.

Shops like Amazon, on the other hand, make money both from people clicking on your Ad and from shoppers actually buying your product. So, they must also take this into account.

That is why one of the most common complaints among Amazon advertisers is that their products never show up: Amazon focuses on products with a higher chance of leading to a sale.

Here are the components Google's ranking algorithm uses to determine your ranking, ordered by importance (source: NeilPatel.com).

- Trust/authority of the host domain: 24%
- Link popularity of the specific page: 22%
- Anchor text of external links to the page: 20%
- On-page keyword usage: 15%
- Registration and hosting data: 7%
- Traffic and click-through rate: 6%
- Social graph metrics: 5%

SEARCH ENGINE OPTIMISATION (SEO)

Now that the importance of ranking highly is clear, the next obvious question is: **what can you do to rank higher?**

The answer, of course, is to optimize your website (or product, on Amazon) so that it achieves a higher ranking. This will give it extra visibility on search engines, allowing you to appear before your competitors.

This optimisation process is called **Search Engine Optimization** or **SEO**.

WHAT DO SEARCH ENGINES LOOK FOR?

To optimise a website, you must first understand how search engines rank websites. Ranking is calculated based on dozens of factors, including how old the website's name is, how much content it has, how many people refer to it, how long people visit for, how many people visit it, and more.

KEYWORDS AND RELEVANT CONTENT

While factors like domain authority and video content are important, the most important thing search engines are looking for is **quality content**.

Keywords play a big part in quality content. Simply put, **keywords are the terms people search for**. It's what people type into Google. For example, how did you find this book? Probably by searching Google or Amazon for writing tips, copywriting, or for Rayne's name. If so, then we were successful in choosing a book title and description which includes the kind of keywords that people search for.

Likewise, keywords play a big part in SEO. Websites depend on them to rank higher for the right searches. That's why, while most websites often include off-topic content, people generally want to keep all the content they post relevant to the overall keywords covered on their site.

INCOMING, OUTGOING, AND INTERNAL LINKS

So-called **backlinks** are the second major part of SEO. Backlinks, or **incoming links**, refer to any link that is pointing back at your site.

While, generally speaking, the more links which point to a website, the higher its ranking, not all links are the same. Links from high-quality websites boost your reputation much more than those from low-quality ones.

So-called **outgoing links** are important, too. If you never link anywhere, Google will assume your content is not worth ranking. Quality content will include citations, i.e. links to the source of the information.

Internal links matter, too. When you link to your other content, you help Google navigate your site. Not only will Google then understand your site a little better, you will also encourage your visitors to spend more time on your website—another indicator of a quality website.

SO... WHAT IS SEO?

All of this. Keywords, relevant content, links—are all part of search engine optimization. However, at its most basic, you can boil it down to this: **be concise, be consistent, be specific.**

If you are **concise** about your site's topic, **consistently** delivering content into the world, and **specific** when it comes to your goals and who your audience is, you will succeed in SEO!

TERMS USED IN THIS CHAPTER

Auction model: The process by which search engines and social media choose which Ad to display on your SERP or timeline.

Keywords: The terms people search for on search engines.

Ranking: A number that search engines and social media assign to Ads and websites to know which ones should be prioritized on SERP.

Organic results: Results on a SERP that are not paid for by a company or marketer.

SERP: Search Engine Results Page. The page you see after running a search. It includes the results of your search and—usually—sponsored content and Ads.

NOVICE MISTAKE TO AVOID

The most common mistake people make with SEO is to **write for search engines instead of readers**. While it is important to tweak your copy in a way that takes SEO into account, it is even more important to write in a clear way which your readers will understand. This actually helps from an SEO point of view even more than keyword-stuffing, as search engines take into account how long people spend on your website.

INSIDER TIP

A post's address (or URL, or slug) to posts, pages, and products in your store also play a part in SEO. If you wish to rank for a specific keyword, **add it in the slug**. Search engines will then rank you higher for that keyword.

RAYNE'S EXPERIENCE

In their quest for SEO, clients can make bizarre requests. Several clients wo hired me to write listicles wanted the current trending keywords to be the 'best' (easiest, safest, tastiest, healthiest, most recommended, most shocking, most romantic) items. This could lead to dilemmas when I had personal experience with that product or place and knew that it was far from easy or safe.

Sometimes the item didn't even exist. A travel organisation requested a listicle 'Twelve Historical Buildings in Paris You Must Visit'. I accepted the job, since I'd been to Paris and could recommend several houses worth seeing. But the client gave me a list of all the places which most people searched for at the time. This included the Bastille. Ahem... The Bastille can't be visited because it was demolished in 1789.

ASSIGNMENT

Run a Google search for a keyword of your choice. As you type it in, notice Google's suggestions: these are a great way of coming up with ideas for a blog post that will feature that keyword. Write them down.

After you press Enter, notice at the bottom of the SERP the "People also ask" section. This is another way to come up with ideas and "hot" questions. Write them down as well.

Now, use these keywords and questions to write two paragraphs on the keyword of your choice. Title each with one of the questions people ask. Repeat your keyword at least twice in each paragraph.

CHAPTER 22

MORE THAN KEYWORDS: THE SECRETS OF SEO COPYWRITING

Nicholas C Rossis

SEO copywriting is a specialised form of online writing, SEO standing for **Search Engine Optimised (spelled 'optimized' in American English).**

While copywriting in general aims at producing engaging material that readers will enjoy, SEO copywriting combines this goal with the need to drive traffic to the article or post you're writing.

In practice, this requires the article to rank highly on search engines, something achieved by:

- Using the right keywords and key phrases.
- Having the right number of words.
- Writing an authoritative article (as measured by links).
- Keeping readers engaged.
- Formatting your page the right way.
- Using the right meta data.

This chapter examines these requirements in detail, one by one, starting with keywords and keyphrases.

KEYWORDS AND KEYPHRASES

On-page keyword usage matters to search engines—a lot. **A full 15% of determining a page's Google ranking comes from keywords.**

Keyword Research

Many clients will give you a **brief** where they list the keywords and keyphrases they want included in the article. They usually highlight a single one as the focus of the post and ask you to include as many of the rest as you can.

I can't stress how important it is to **follow the brief to the letter**. A keyphrase such as "What is SEO copywriting?" is different from "SEO copywriting tips." Keyword research is a science in itself and the client has chosen the focus keyphrase in accordance with the rest of their promotion efforts. Your article is only one piece of a 1000-piece puzzle you are not even aware of. So, while creativity with titles is wonderful, do **not** exercise it unless the client indicates it is okay to do so.

Preparing The Brief

If the client simply indicates the topic in general instead of producing a brief, then you must conduct the keyword research and prepare the brief yourself. While you can use some extremely useful specialized tools such as SEMRush and AppSumo's Frase, the easiest way to do this is to go to Google and type the keyphrase into the search field.

As soon as you start typing, you will see that Google comes up with **suggestions** underneath. These indicate **high-volume searches** and are a good starting point for your article. Jot them down to use them as chapter titles.

When you hit "Enter," Google will display the results. Scroll all the way to the bottom and look for the "**Searches related to**…" section.

You will see underneath two columns of similar searches. These are excellent for providing content and keyword ideas. Try to include them verbatim in your copy. If you are still short on keywords, follow the links and note the searches related to them as well.

Number Of Words

While you're still on Google's results page, visit the top three results and see how many words these articles have. To compete, aim at writing **20% more words** than the top one. For example, if the top three articles have 500, 600, and 800 words respectively, try to write 1,000 words to ensure that your article shows up above them.

Again, keep in mind that this is more of a guideline. **The number of words matters—but so does readability**. Writing long copy that is both concise and engaging is a challenge that separates good SEO copywriters from poor ones.

One solution is to **use how-tos and tips**. I once wrote a 3,000-words article on plumbing. When I first heard the word count, I was speechless. How on earth would I write 3,000 words on plumbing?

Strangely enough, the article proved fun to write, as it explained all the different kinds of plumbing services my client undertook. These included septic tank installation and repair, video inspections, portable toilet rentals, drains, cisterns, boilers, faucets, and even water coolers. Each of these had its own section. Each section included a paragraph with maintenance tips for trouble-free usage, leading to a surprisingly popular article. Who doesn't want to know how to avoid plumbing trouble in their homes?

Using Keywords

Now that you have the keywords and target word-count, it is time to get started on the copy. Use the keywords and keyphrases throughout your copy. Also, remember the related searches mentioned above? Include these verbatim in your text to maximise the number of popular searches your article will display for.

When using keywords, one common mistake is **keyword stuffing**. Use the keywords as naturally as possible. You're writing for readers; not machines. Some writers go as far as to prepare the first draft of the copy paying scant attention to keywords, focusing instead on creating engaging content. The second draft is where they optimise the copy for SEO purposes.

Even so, it can be easy to get carried away when writing for a specific keyword and use it every other sentence. However, this soon becomes counterproductive. While Google uses keywords to gauge what a particular web page is about, it is also smart and will penalise you for any real or perceived attempt to trick it. Use SEO Scout's free keyword analyser or a plugin like Yoast to make sure you are not keyword-stuffing your copy.

LINK BUILDING

Links to a page is the second big factor influencing its ranking. No less than **20% of the page's ranking depends on links**. However, not all links are the same. Search engines also look at the so-called **anchor text**—the text used as a link.

For example, consider these two links:

- To find out more about <u>SEO copywriting</u>, click here.
- To find out more about SEO copywriting, <u>click here</u>.

The first link tells Google that the page you're linking to is about SEO copywriting. When someone searches for the keyphrase, "SEO copywriting," Google will know this is a relevant page.

The second link tells Google that the page you're linking to is about "click here." Google will probably ignore it, as it could link to pretty much anything.

That is why it's so important to phrase your links the right way. To maximise the link's benefit, use a popular search phrase. In our example, you could phrase this as follows:

"[What is SEO copywriting?](#) Find out here."

This ensures that your page will be considered by Google every time someone asks that common question.

Links on a page can lead to either another page on your website or an external resource. These two are **not** the same.

Links To External Websites

When you link to an external website, you add to your own authority. It means that you have done your research and are linking to your sources. This kind of link acts as a citation, telling Google that you are trustworthy—as long as the destination link is also a trustworthy destination.

Add a couple of links to such sites as part of your copy. If you need to add more, however, do so **at the end** of the copy in the form of a list of references. Any link to an outside source means a potentially lost reader. This way, you both link to high-authority websites and keep your audience at your website until they finish reading.

Internal Links

An internal link is any link from one page on your website to another page on your website. While menu links are also internal links, links that are part of your copy are called **contextual links**.

Search engines use contextual links to create a structure of your website. For example, a post that is linked to from several others is treated as a **cornerstone** post and may come up higher in searches.

Google usually places greater value on the home page, followed by newer content. A simple way to promote a post is by linking to it from the home page. Additionally, you can promote older content if you edit and repost it, as Google will treat it as fresh content. Finally, adding a **related posts** section also helps promote your other posts without you having to lift a finger.

One last thing you can do is use a plugin that automatically generates a **table of contents** based on the copy's headings. This creates internal links which help search engines understand your copy's structure and rank your page higher.

KEEPING READERS ENGAGED

Did you know that the average reading age of the UK population is 9 years—that is, they have the reading ability normally expected of a 9-year-old? As for the US, it is equivalent to a 7th/8th grader (12 to 14 years old).

I don't care if you have a Ph.D., SEO copywriting is **not** the place for you to show off your knowledge. As Dale Carnegie once pointed out, we may love strawberry tarts but when we go fishing, we use worms as bait. Tailor your copy to your audience and be realistic about who they are.

To maximise the readability of your copy:

- **Keep your sections short**—up to three paragraphs each.
- Use **headings** to create a clear structure of your copy. Start with heading 2 (as heading 1 is reserved for the title) and continue up to heading 4 as necessary.
- **Keep your paragraphs short**—under five lines each.
- **Keep your sentences short**. Use punctuation to separate longer sentences (see what I did there?).
- Avoid **overrun sentences**.
- Use **lists**, **bold** elements, and **blockquotes** to break up the text. People skim over long lines of text and read long copy in an F-shaped pattern (Nielsen, 2006). Helps the reader's gaze rest on the parts you wish to emphasise by using different kinds of formatting to breaking up your text.

A great trick to increase engagement is to use anecdotes and stories. Despite what you may think, **story-telling** is a great tool in business writing as we all love stories and find them relatable.

Fiction has been used in business articles for decades to engage the audience. The Wall Street Journal once published an article titled "two young men." In it, they wrote a fictional account of two young men who joined the same company at the same age. One ended up as a manager while the other became the president.

The article turned out to be such a success that it has been used for the past three decades to teach and inspire young business professionals.

PAGE FORMATTING

The above covers readability—the copywriting part of SEO copywriting. Here are some tips to cover the SEO part of it:

- Include the primary keyword in the **title**. If this is a keyphrase given to you by the client, use it verbatim, even if it's grammatically incorrect.

- Include the primary keyword in the **first paragraph**.

- Include the primary keyword in a **subheading**.

- Include the primary keyword in your **copy** while avoiding **overstuffing**.

- Include the primary keyword in your **conclusion**.

- Include the primary keyword in your **CTA**.

META DATA

When optimizing an article for SEO purposes, plugins like Yoast ask for meta data. Use these to maximize the SEO impact.

Your meta tags should be unique to each page and highly relevant to the content on the page. Avoid using a blanket statement that could go on each page with small modifications.

The main meta data are:

- Meta title,
- meta description,
- slug (URL),
- and image metadata

These are examined in detail below.

Meta Title

The main purpose of the meta title is to make someone want to click on it when they see it in the search results. It should, therefore, **always include the target keyword**. When character count permits, add extra (key)words to make it more appealing. It should be unique, i.e. different from the article's title.

Meta Description

Essentially, this has the same guidelines as the meta title, except you have more characters to play with. The opening paragraph of an article may give you some ideas for the meta description (and often serves as a search snippet for Google).

Follow the tips below to create the perfect meta description:

- Do **not** use keyword meta descriptions for the sake of keywording as this can lead to keyword stuffing very quickly.
- Use **synonyms** of the main keywords, provided those keywords closely follow the content of the page itself.

- Follow the recommended **character counts**—around **150** at the time of writing. However, if you go slightly over, that is fine, too.

- Avoid **generalised meta descriptions** and hollow phrases such as "best widgets" and other sales speak. This turns off prospective customers. Speak about what your readers are really after, instead of talking them into a sale.

Think about meta titles and descriptions from the perspective of conversions: what will entice a reader to click through to the website? Sometimes, it may even be appropriate to include a phone number and end with a **CTA**. For example:

"Did you know that SEO copywriting can drive traffic to your website without paying for ads? Learn how in our latest blog post or call 123457890 to increase your sales without paying a dime."

The above has 155 characters. Importantly, it includes both a CTA and a phone number—useful if someone is reading on their phone—and works even if the last part is truncated.

Slug (URL)

The slug is the last part of the web address and should focus on the **main keywords**. Drop any conjunctions, articles, and prepositions. So, if your title and keyphrase are "The Majority of People Now Read Online," the slug should be "people-read-online."

Images and image metadata

Images are an integral part of the article—and SEO. When downloading an image, save it with a name that includes your target keywords.

Image meta data such as the **title** and **description** are used by search engines and visually impaired people using screen radars (software that reads out loud anything on a web page).

My metadata usually consists of **two parts** separated by a pipe character (|). The first part is a **description** of the image (keyword-rich, if possible). The second may include the post title, the company name, and a brief description of what it does. This is where I insert any keywords my client consistently wishes to rank higher for. I insert this text into both the Description and Title fields but **not in the Caption** field to avoid it appearing on the page.

NOVICE MISTAKE TO AVOID

Don't write for search engines.

Quality has become the #1 ranking factor in Google, especially since the Google Panda and Penguin updates. Google measures this by checking how long your visitors stay on your website after clicking on a link. If they leave right away because of dreadful copy (or any other reason), your article's ranking will drop immediately, no matter how optimised is it for SEO purposes.

INSIDER TIPS

Use a tool like SEOScout's free keyword analyser to check the keyword density in your copy. If you are writing an article for WordPress, use one of the many plugins, like Yoast, to check your copy for the keyword or keyphrase in question. Unlike what many seem to think, these tools do **not** optimise your copy. They point out areas of improvement so that **you** can optimise it.

Also, as we saw, Google measures how much time a visitor spends on your page. Every second counts, especially with competitive keywords. Besides great copy, use video, images, infographics, and story-telling to increase reader engagement. Anything that can keep your readers longer on your page is good!

ASSIGNMENT

Find a topic of interest and keyword-research it. Create a brief that includes these three sections:

- Related searches
- Similar articles
- Number of words

Next, write an article following the guidelines listed here and including the metadata. Download an image from pixabay.com and insert it into your copy. Finally, use SEO Scout (https://seoscout.com/tools/keyword-analyzer) to keyword-analyse your copy and make any changes necessary.

Bonus assignment: find a website or blog that specialises in your subject and offer your article as a free guest post. Congratulations, you've just taken your first step in becoming a fully-fledged SEO copywriter by building up your portfolio!

CHAPTER 23

THEIR RULES, NOT YOURS: ABIDING BY HOUSE STYLES

Nicholas C Rossis

A lawyer client once asked me to write a post for his blog. I was happy to oblige and checked his website to get an idea of the style he preferred. His posts were so dry I almost reached for my eye drops. Even worse, he paid so little consideration to SEO practices that I wondered if he was deliberately trying to escape Google's attention.

I merrily sat down to fix all these problems with my brilliant SEO copywriting. I researched the subject he had provided me with and wrote a post that not only explained everything in simple English, perfect for the layperson, but was also packed with SEO goodness. It was fun, exciting, and ended with a lovely CTA.

My client hated it so much that he complained to the agency that had got me the job.

You see, I had broken the most basic rule of copywriting: you're not writing for yourself; you're writing for your client. Or, as my father used to say, "**My house, my rules**."

WRITING STYLES

My mistake was basically one of arrogance. I genuinely thought that I knew better and wrote according to the two pillars of good SEO copywriting:

- All copy should be **readable**
- Blog posts should be **optimised** for search engines.

Unfortunately, it turns out there's a third pillar—one I had ignored: **you must write in your client's style.**

Since then, I have added a new section to the questionnaire I send new clients:

Your post should be: warm, friendly, professional, trustworthy, fun, sophisticated, formal, enthusiastic.

Each adjective comes with a tickbox so that I know what style to follow.

(For more about this, see Rayne's chapter about 'The Client's Voice'.)

HOUSE RULES SUCK. SO WHAT?

What should you do if you feel very strongly that a client's style sucks?

Follow it.

Your client may have a dozen other considerations that you are not aware of. They may wish to impress the CEO or their peers. Their posts may be part of an entire marketing strategy. Or they may simply have different tastes than you.

That's why you don't have the right to unilaterally make up your own rules and ignore theirs. For better or worse, **you're a pen for hire** and should strive to mimic your client's voice as closely as possible.

If you can't do that, then it's best to simply pass that job to someone who's a better fit for it. I am lucky enough to have writer friends who take on projects for me when I'm swamped. One of them has had law training. In the case of my lawyer client, I explained my predicament and asked her to write the next post on my behalf. Unsurprisingly, the client liked that second post much better—thus saving my relationship with the agent who had got me the job.

DIFFICULT CLIENTS

Some clients are difficult. They will micromanage you (a pet hate of mine), question every word choice, and ask for counter-intuitive edits, like removing crucial keywords and gutting your copy's SEO in the process.

You have every right to point out that, if you do as they ask, your copy won't be optimised for search engines or will be hard to read. **Warn them about that in a polite email.** That way, they can't turn around a few months later and accuse you of writing copy that failed to generate organic leads.

- Start your email by **thanking** them for their feedback.
- **Accept** any suggestions that won't affect SEO.
- Then, **ask** them respectfully to reconsider the parts that do. Explain how, in your professional experience, those suggestions might result in a loss of organic traffic or in hard-to-read copy.
- Close your email by acknowledging that they have taken time off their busy schedule to work on the post with you. **Thank** them for that.

After that, it's up to them.

Rayne has written a chapter about 'Dealing with Difficult Clients' to help you with prevent problems and handle tricky situations.

BRITISH VS AMERICAN ENGLISH

During the early stages of the Battle of the Bulge, the Germans assembled an army of impostors for a top-secret mission known as Operation Greif. A handful of English-speaking German soldiers were outfitted with captured American weapons, jeeps and uniforms before slipping behind the U.S. lines and posing as G.I.s.

While their actual acts of sabotage might better be described as a series of frat pranks, such as switching road signs, they were pretty successful at spreading confusion. G.I.s set up checkpoints and began grilling passersby on baseball and American pop culture to confirm their identities. The results were often farcical, as when one overzealous American G.I. detained General Bradley for a few hours after he answered that the capital of Illinois was Springfield: the soldier incorrectly believed it was Chicago.

This episode highlights the importance of **localisation**. We use countless minute signals to read between the lines in our interactions with others. I'm based in the UK and it turns out that this psychological fact influences not just grammar but also my entire writing style.

When I write for British clients, I use British English. When I write for Americans, I use American English. There are some differences in grammar and vocabulary but nothing so major that it becomes an issue.

It's the style differences that trip me up—what I call **the Bulge effect**. Since most of my clients are Americans, I seem to be caught somewhere between the two cultures. Incidentally, this has the funny consequence of my American clients sometimes assuming I am Canadian. Eh?

Adding to the complexity is the fact that the US is a pretty big place. Each state has its own traditions, idioms, and expressions. If you say "y'all," you're revealing yourself to be from the South. Saying "bless your heart" sounds lovely in England. Coming from an American Southerner, it means that you're an idiot—but what can you do. And if someone's drunk, would you say he's "three sheets to the wind," "sloshed," "hammered," or "wasted"? Each of these reveals you to be from a different part of the English-speaking world.

To me, this is one of the most challenging aspects of the job. I can study grammar and learn when to use "sidewalk" instead of "pavement." But the more localised nuances sometimes escape me. I once used the word "smashing" a couple of times in a meeting, thus inadvertently revealing myself as a non-American. Thankfully, no one minded—they just had a chuckle at my odd choice of word.

GRAMMAR RULES

When hired by a new client, ask if they have a **style manual**. Many businesses nowadays compile a document with **style guidelines** that you must follow. These usually cover things like formatting and grammar. For example:

- How should you capitalise titles?
- Should you use bold or italics for emphasis?
- Do they want bullet lists?
- Should links open in new tabs?
- How long should paragraphs be?
- Is jargon encouraged or discouraged?
- Oxford comma: blessing or anathema?
- To hyphenate or not to hyphenate?

It can be confusing having to remember each client's style but it's an essential part of writing—and their editor will thank you instead of, well, blessing your heart.

WRITING STYLES

Most businesses and organizations follow one of four style guides. The AP style's origins lie in journalism, so it's used in most media. The APA, Chicago, and MLA have academic origins and are used widely within academia. However, several journalistic and publishing media with no relation to academia prefer their style guides to AP.

Check with your client to see what their preferred style is:

- **Associated Press Stylebook (AP Style).** AP style provides consistent guidelines for the content of newspapers and other mass media in terms of grammar, spelling, punctuation, and language usage.
- **Chicago Manual of Style (CMOS, or Chicago Style).** Created by the University of Chicago, it was originally used mainly in papers and student essays but has now expanded to copywriting as well.
- **American Psychological Association Style (APA Style).** Used mainly to cite sources within the social sciences.
- **The Modern Language Association (MLA Style).** Also an academic style guide resource, it is addressed primarily to secondary-school and undergraduate college and university teachers and students.

It should be noted that several publications, e.g. The Economist, have developed their own style guides. If you are ever lucky enough to write for any of them, be sure to follow them.

NOVICE MISTAKES TO AVOID

Don't think you know better than your client. You don't. And whatever you do, never antagonise your client. **Arguing with a client and trying to prove that you're right will only generate ill will and jeopardise your professional reputation.** It's *never* worth it. If you're not a good fit, asking for help or passing on the job are both fine options. Trying to change your client's mind is not.

INSIDER TIPS

Watching movies and reading plenty of books and blogs is the best solution to the problem of localisation.

Also, use your friends. The next best thing to actually living in a place is having friends who do. The internet has brought us all closer together. Take advantage of Zoom and Skype and talk to your friends abroad.

Not only is all this fun, it will helpfully influence your writing style!

RAYNE'S SUGGESTION

I use British English, too. Sometimes, a client wants copy in American English, and I oblige. The differences aren't just in the word choices, but in syntax, grammar, spelling and punctuation, and small variations sometimes slip past me.

Before I submit a piece of writing in American English, I ask a US-American writer friend to check it for me. I return the favour when they need to write in British English.

I recommend that you, too, enlist a 'native' to check your British or American English to get it right.

ASSIGNMENT

Find and write down three key differences between:

- British English and American English
- AP Style and APA Style
- AP Style and Chicago Style
- AP Style and MLA

CHAPTER 24

FIND PICTURES TO SUPPORT YOUR WORDS: SOURCING ILLUSTRATIONS

Nicholas C Rossis

A surprising number of clients expect you to provide visual assets along with your copy such as images.

You have to be extremely careful when submitting images with your article. Clients using images without permission are open to litigation—and so are you. Don't think you can just search Google for your keyword, find any image that appeals to you, and send it to your client. **Ensure that you have the appropriate rights for any image you use**.

Thankfully, dozens of websites provide just that: royalty-free images you can use in your content for free. Several more provide the same at a fee. While the former have the advantage of being, well, free, the latter often offer more specialised material.

LICENCE TYPES

You can only use material that is **free from copyright restrictions**. In other words, you can download and use it for both commercial and personal use. Depending on the circumstances, you may or may not need to attribute or notify the copyright holder.

The two most common types of stock photo licences you'll see are **Royalty-Free** (RF) and **Rights-Managed** (RM).

Royalty-Free

Royalty-free images are not, in fact, free. With these licences, the buyer receives **unlimited usage** from the holder of the copyright once they purchase or download the photo. The buyer can use the image for as long as they like with as many projects as they desire. As long as the buyer stays within the terms of the agreement, all is good.

Rights Managed

With these images, there tends to be **restrictions** regarding when, where, and how the image can be used. The restrictions may have to do with various regions, industries, length of use, etc.

WHAT TO LOOK FOR

Here is what content creators typically look for in the tools they choose to use:

User-Friendliness

An hour spent learning a new tool or platform is an hour not spent writing. You need intuitive tools with a straightforward interface and easy-to-operate features.

Functionality

Most platforms are specialised. For example, Foodiesfeed offers photographs about food, Ancestry Images vintage photos, and Move East Asian photos. Which one you choose depends largely on the subject you write about. This is even more important with a paid subscription. What's the point of paying for a platform that specialises in topics you never cover?

Cost-Effectiveness

Some services are free. Some are reasonably priced. And some are pretty expensive for freelancers. **Unless your client covers**

Copywriting

the cost, don't rush to pay for subscriptions you may rarely use or that are more expensive than you need. A balance has to be maintained; you should return all that you put in with a surplus.

LIST OF STOCK PHOTO RESOURCES

Here are some of the best Royalty-Free sites, organised alphabetically. Whether you're on the hunt for one stellar image or a whole group of them, these resources will help you in your quest to find that perfect photo. From scenic beach shots to styled food spreads, there's something inspiring in this list for every need.

1. Ancestry Images

Ancestry Images (https://www.ancestryimages.com/) is a free image archive of historical prints and images dating from the 17th but mostly from the later 18th century and 19th century.

If it's history you're after, Ancestry Images offers a free image archive of historical prints. It's an image resource made especially for historians, genealogists, and those interested in diving into family history, local history, or ancestry.

2. Bossfight

BossFight (https://bossfight.co/) aggregates photos daily from other popular free photo download sites that are free of restrictions. You can download photos individually, subscribe for free, or get a downloadable zip file of every image once a month.

3. Bucketlistly

Bucketlistly (https://photos.bucketlistly.com/) contains 2800+ travel photos categorized by country.

4. Fancy Crave

Fancy Crave (https://fancycrave.com/) offers 14 free, high resolution, professional, and emotionally driven photos weekly.

From typewriters to horses, to office spaces — you'll surely find something unique to fit your project.

5. Find a Photo

Find a Photo (https://www.chamberofcommerce.org/findaphoto) specialises in search-by-colour images — from blues to purples to pinks and more. In addition, you can choose by collection (like wild animals, light rays, landmarks, bokeh, etc.).

6. FoodiesFeed

Just as the name suggests, **FoodiesFeed** (https://www.foodiesfeed.com/) is devoted to all things food. It offers thousands of high resolution, mouth-watering shots, along with and free digital goods related to food.

7. Free Nature Stock

Free Nature Stock (https://freenaturestock.com/) is the ultimate stock photography destination for nature lovers. If you're looking for royalty-free nature stock photos that you can use however you'd like, the site is photo gold. Created by Adrian Pelletier and updated daily, it features stars, sunsets, mountains, and everything in between.

8. Gratisography

Gratisography (https://gratisography.com/) offers free images for your own personal and commercial use. Photos are added weekly by Ryan McGuire of Bells Design and are free of copyright restrictions.

9. ISO Republic

ISO Republic (https://isorepublic.com) offers free stock photos for creative professionals. From animals to people, food, and drink, they cover a wide variety of cool, shareable images.

10. Life of Pix

With no copyright restrictions, **Life of Pix** (https://www.lifeofpix.com) offers fresh, innovative photos from the Leeroy creative agency. In addition, they feature a photographer of the week to ignite inspiration.

11. Magdeleine

Magdeleine (https://magdeleine.co/browse/) offers free, hand-picked photos filled with inspiration. Browse through peaceful images of flowers, coffee cups, snow-dusted trees, and more.

12. Minimography

Minimography (https://minimography.com/) specialises in trendy, royalty-free, minimalist photos.

13. Morgue File

Despite the morbid name, **Morgue File** (https://morguefile.com) offers free images for creatives, by creatives. To keep the inspiration flowing, they host a daily photo challenge called #quest, which sends creatives out into the world on assignment to capture various elements of life unfolding around them.

14. Move East

Move East (https://moveast.me/) covers the journeys in Asia of João Pacheco, a Portuguese man on the move. He decided every image should be used for free and as such, you're allowed to use his scenic, breath-taking photos however (and wherever) you'd like.

15. New Old Stock

If you're looking to recapture history and tell your own story, check out **New Old Stock's** (https://nos.twnsnd.co/) vintage photos from the public archives. They are free of known copyright restrictions and feature everything from old offices and city streets to people and restaurants. Just beware — they are also a great way to pass your time scrolling through them!

16. Pexels

Pexels (https://www.pexels.com/) offers one of the greatest selections of royalty-free photos online. With a touch of romance and whimsy, it offers approachable, hip, and colour-filled images. Find everything from engagement shots and cookie spreads to sleepy cats.

17. Picjumbo

From fashion to nature, **Picjumbo** (https://picjumbo.com) offers free images for all your stock photo needs. Fresh images are added every day, which means you have a great chance of finding something that suits your creative needs.

18. Picography

Submitted by Dave Meier (and other photographers), the beautiful photos on **Picography** (https://picography.co) range from holiday snapshots to scenic landscape images. They're free and released under the Creative Commons CC0 Licence (https://creativecommons.org/publicdomain/zero/1.0/).

19. Pikwizard

If it's **photos of people** you're looking for, then **Pikwizard** (https://pikwizard.com) is the perfect resource for you. All photos are free to use without attribution. Pikwizard has over 100,000 completely free images on the site, over 20,000 of which are exclusive to it. They're also adding new images to their library daily since their ultimate goal is to get to more than 1 million images.

20. Pixabay

Pixabay (https://pixabay.com/) is another one of the biggest providers of stock photos. With 1.3 million images, it offers photographs, illustrations, vector graphics, and more.

21. RBGstock

One of the largest collections of free high-quality photographs, **RGB Stock** (https://www.rgbstock.com/) is searchable by tag or category. Photos are free of copyright restrictions.

22. Skitter Photo

Skitter Photo (https://skitterphoto.com/) images can be used by anyone for any purpose. Find cityscapes, streets lined with fallen orange leaves, macro shots of coffee beans, car snaps, and a whole lot more.

23. StockSnap

StockSnap (https://stocksnap.io) features free, high-resolution stock images. It tracks downloads so you can see what's most popular and adds images daily. All photos are Creative Commons public domain.

24. The Pattern Library

The Pattern Library (https://thepatternlibrary.com/) offers an assortment of free, creative patterns for all your design needs. From 'kale salad' to 'flowers' to 'the illusionist,' use these patterns to add flair and funk to your site or project.

25. Travel Coffee Book

The **Travel Coffee Book** (https://travelcoffeebook.com/) offers a large collection of travel photos from different destinations. Venture from the streets of China to the foods of Thailand to the sunsets of Croatia and beyond.

26. Unsplash

Unsplash (https://unsplash.com/) is the third big name in the world of free stock photos. It provides an incredible collection of high-resolution stock images, from blog-worthy family shots to food photos. The best images are featured on the homepage and all are released for free under Unsplash's licence. If you're looking for HDR images, in particular, they have a nice assortment of landscape and city shots.

27. Visual Hunt

Visual Hunt (https://visualhunt.com/) is an aggregator that curates the best free images from many online sources and pulls them together. Why browse one site at the time when you can search them all with one click?

PAID RESOURCES

While free stock photos will cover most of your needs, there are times when the perfect photo proves elusive. Popular resources that aren't free but can help you find the right photo for your photo include:

500px

500px (https://500px.com/) offers mobile professionals and photographers the chance to share their products and their photography online. In their marketplace, they offer premium royalty-free stock photos from over 8 million top photographers (and they're incredible).

Flickr

Flickr (https://www.flickr.com/) is home to tens of billions of photos — and lots of Flickr users offer their work under a Creative Commons License.

iStock

iStock by Getty Images (https://istock.com/) offers flexible plans and pricing for photos, illustrations, auto, and video. Browse through patterns and backgrounds, templates, infographics, and more, until you find just what you're looking for.

Shutterstock

Shutterstock (https://www.shutterstock.com/) is one of the most popular sites for stock photography. It offers an incredible variety of images (including 10,000 new photos per day) and once you purchase a plan, the world is your oyster.

StoryBlocks

Storyblocks (https://www.storyblocks.com/ — formerly Graphicstock) offers great value for money. Download as many images as you like for a small annual fee.

Stock Photo Secrets

Stock Photo Secrets (https://www.stockphotosecrets.com/best-stock-photo-sites) is a list with stock photo sites, updated for 2020.

NOVICE MISTAKES TO AVOID

Whatever you do, **never use an image without checking the copyright first**! Not only does this make you look unprofessional, but it can also lead to litigation for you and your client.

Also, **don't waste too much time searching for photos**. It is only too easy to get distracted by pretty images, to the point of forgetting why you went there in the first place!

INSIDER TIP

Personally, I check **Pixabay** first when I need an image. If I can't find what I'm looking for, I use my **Shutterstock** subscription. This combination takes minutes of my time, has rarely let me down, and costs a reasonable $35 per month.

RAYNE'S SUGGESTIONS

Don't automatically reach for stock images. Real photos taken by the client may not dazzle with technical perfection, but their authenticity makes them more interesting,

Instead of yet another boring posed picture of implausibly handsome professional models posing with implausible white-toothed smiles in an immaculate office, show the client's real team at work.

This works especially well for blog and social media posts where authenticity and a personal touch matter more than technical brilliance.

When using stock images, clarify who is paying for them—the client or you? If you have a monthly subscription to a service, like Nicholas has, that's no problem. But if the photos need to be paid for individually, this can cost you more than you're earning from the copywriting job.

ASSIGNMENT

While it may be relatively easy to find an image for an item (e.g. "laptop") and certain concepts (e.g. "wedding"), technical photos (e.g. "CBD extraction") can be harder.

Choose a concept and search for it on Visual Hunt, Pixabay, Pexels, Unsplash, Shutterstock, and iStockPhoto. What differences and similarities do you notice in the various websites' approach?

CHAPTER 25

THE PLACE WHERE IT HAPPENS: OPTIMISING THE LANDING PAGE

Nicolas C Rossis

A landing page is the very first page prospective customers will see when they click the client's Ad. Most people will visit it with only a vague interest in the product. It is up to the landing page to turn them into **paying** customers—which makes writing copy for a landing page particularly tricky.

To achieve a high conversion rate, everything on the product page should be tailored to the target audience, building up their enthusiasm in the product or service and encouraging them to make a purchase.

Let's use the example of **wireless speakers** to see how we could build a landing page for the Ad we created in the chapter 'Writing Ad Copy'.

CONTENTS OF A LANDING PAGE

A landing page must satisfy two needs:

- It must come up on searches.
- It must turn visitors into paying customers.

Unfortunately, these are often in conflict. For example, you may need 3,000 words to ensure search engine visibility. However, shorter copy will likely convert better.

The answer is to **divide your copy into smaller sections**.

Generally speaking, a landing page may contain any or all of the following sections:

- A section explaining the product's main value
- Several value statements
- Three focus points
- Videos
- Reviews and testimonials
- Numbers and statistics (e.g. "10,000 satisfied customers," "150 years in business," "1,000 units installed," etc.)
- A section describing how the advertised product or service will improve the customer's life

Scattered throughout the page should also be CTAs—buttons that let eager customers place an order (explained in detail in the chapter 'The Call to Action').

TITLE

Every page starts with a **title**. Think of yours as a hook. Use it to entice customers to shop while also letting them know they are on the right page. You can achieve this by giving the product an appropriate title. If your speakers are called XYZ, title your product page, "Enjoy the best music with XYZ Wireless Speakers." This will help both search engines and shoppers know what the product is, while also describing a pleasant experience from the outset.

PRODUCT DESCRIPTION

This should come right after the title, as it is what most people interested in the product will want to know. Make it clear from the very first paragraph what the product is and what it does. In order to buy something, people must first understand what it is. This is not the place to sell or use evocative words, it is a place that will let customers know they've come to the right place.

Use as simple terms as possible and repeat your core **keywords** here—in this case, wireless speakers. This will encourage search engines to display your product first on their results.

FULFIL A NEED

Once that crucial first paragraph is written, it is now time to expand. Start by identifying the **need** the product will fulfil. In our example, this may be the need to share your music with others.

Offer **specific examples** to cover as many scenarios as possible. For instance, mention how a wireless speaker will help you and your friends listen to music at the beach, park, or home.

Make sure to portray the product as the perfect answer to this need and a sale is almost guaranteed.

MENTION THE CLIENT'S UNIQUE SELLING POINTS (USP)

The next question in a customer's mind will be, "that's great, but I've also found a similar product that's much cheaper. Why should I buy this one?"

Pre-empt this question by explaining why shoppers should prefer your client's product instead of a competitor's. This is particularly important with more expensive items, as many people will naturally prefer the cheapest alternative if all else is (or seems to be) equal.

So, what sets your client's speakers apart from the rest? The Unique Selling Point (USP) may be higher technical specifications or excellent after-sale service. Show people why the client's product is superior.

SHOW REVIEWS AND TESTIMONIALS

Reviews and **testimonials** can help you secure a sale at this stage. Use them to strengthen your client's USP. For example, someone may have left a review commenting on the high quality of the sound (confirming the USP about the technical qualifications). Another may have shared how you fixed their speakers after they accidentally ran them over repeatedly with a steamroller (now, *that's* excellent after-sales service).

If the product has just been released and has no reviews, your clients may factor this into their promotional strategy. For example, they may decide to run a giveaway to garner more reviews before they spend money on Ads.

USE FAQS

Frequently Asked Questions (FAQs) are a great way to explain the needs that the product will fulfil. Use them not only to answer any questions people may have about your client's product, but also to establish your brand's superiority. For example, even if no one has ever asked how these wireless speakers compare to a well-known brand, write up a question about that and explain how this product is superior. You are the one choosing the questions that will be answered, so use that power intelligently.

SELL AN EXPERIENCE

A perfect page will be about more than the product. It will be about the experience.

As a rule, don't sell a product. Sell an experience.

Have you seen Amazon's Kindle product pages? They are chockfull of technical specifications and comparison tables, showing photos of various Kindle models from several angles. However, they also feature people reading their books in beautiful surroundings, evoking memories of holidays and feelings of relaxation.

NOVICE MISTAKES TO AVOID

As said at the start, a landing page must both be search-engine-friendly and turn visitors into paying customers. When a client asks for a 3,000-words landing page, however, you are no longer writing for customers; you're writing for search engines. And that can lead to an endless sheet of text—a big mistake for a page that's supposed to convert visitors into shoppers.

When your copy is still too long after dividing it into smaller sections, suggest to your client to demarcate sections with titles and subtitles, different background colours, videos, and images. This will break up the page into clearly defined areas that won't confound the eye.

Speaking of images, even though you are a copywriter, don't hesitate to advise your client about the importance of using **professional images** on the landing page. Images are quicker to scan than words, so most people's eyes will fall on the product image first. However, while photos can make a great first impression, they must be crisp and enticing to do so.

If even that fails, suggest to your client to place some sections (e.g. the FAQ) under so-called **accordion** sections—sections that expand to display the text but remain otherwise hidden away, with only the title showing at first.

Whatever you do, don't fill a landing page with long, unbroken paragraphs of plain copy. Nothing drives people away faster than that!

INSIDER TIP

Some clients will ask you to write reviews of their products. A few may offer to send you a sample so you can try it for yourself but most will simply ask you to write a fake review. Personally, I have declined to do so, as this feels to me like I'm lying to people.

However, it is up to you to figure out the best way to handle this. (Rayne has written a chapter about ethics of copywriting, to help you decide what you are and aren't willing to do.)

RAYNE'S SUGGESTION

Landing pages are not always desirable. When you have hooked potential customers, whetting their attention, interest and desire, and they're ready to buy, it's best to lead them directly to a sales page where they can complete the purchase. If you have to visit a landing page first, and then perhaps carry out further clicks to reach the 'Buy Now' button, they often lose interest along the way.

If the client wants or needs a landing page, write the copy for it. But don't urge your client to have landing pages if it doesn't bring genuine benefits.

ASSIGNMENTS

This is for your hypothetical client, the company selling wireless speakers.

- Write five questions and answers about wireless speakers for an FAQ section that will be part of the copy for a landing page.
- Come up with two USPs for your wireless speakers.
- Describe two different experiences people can have when using your wireless speakers.

CHAPTER 26

THE ETHICS OF COPYWRITING: DON'T DO A CLIENT'S DIRTY WORK

Rayne Hall

Some clients use copywriters to do their dirty work—tell lies, deceive customers, spread slander, and promote illegal activities. Whatever clients ask you to do, stick to your values and have the courage to say no.

Your ethical standards may differ from mine, and that's okay. But you need to know what they are.

Instead of waiting until you're faced with a moral dilemma, decide beforehand what you are and aren't willing to do. This will make it easier to spot the problem when it arises, and to deal with it on the spot.

Here are some questions to consider:

- Are you willing to promote products and services **of which you personally don't approve**? For example, if you consider gambling morally wrong, will you accept a job promoting online casinos? If you believe in chastity, will you craft copy for a porn website? Will you promote cigarettes as a non-smoker, alcohol as a teetotaller, meat as a vegetarian, conservative politics as a liberal?

- Are you willing to write what the client tells you to, **even if it's an obvious lie**? Are you willing to bend the truth in the client's interest? Will you quote fake statistics?

- Will you **pretend to be someone else** to boost the client's credibility? For example, if the client needs 20 people to comment on the blog, will you create 20 fake identities to leave comments? Will you pretend to be a happy customer to endorse your client's products with fake reviews? Will you pretend to be an unhappy customer to harm your client's competitor's reputation?

- Will you support **a client who pretends to be someone else**? For example, a client who sells educational materials may pretend to be a teacher with fifty years' experience when he is actually a nineteen-year old with no teaching qualifications—will you write a fake bio for him and blog about his alleged classroom memories?

- Will you promote goods and services which are **not in the customers' best interest**? For example, a client may target pensioners and inveigle them to spend their life savings on a product they don't need. Will you craft persuasive texts for this?

MY PERSONAL GUIDELINES

I've set myself a single clear rule: **I will not lie or deceive in any way.**

I measure any prospective job and new assignment against this yardstick. If the gig involves any kind of deceit, for whatever reason, I decline.

FROM MY PERSONAL EXPERIENCE

Most of my copywriting clients are authors and publishers.

Several have asked me to write and post fake Amazon reviews, giving their book 5* ratings and glowing praise. This is dishonest, as well as against Amazon's rules. I won't do it.

Many authors hire me to write compelling author bios for them. That's one of my specialisms. I'm always surprised how many authors pretend to be someone else. A US American pretends to be Tibetan, so his book on Buddhism appears more 'authentic'. A male romance writer pretends to be female, because he believes female-authored romances will sell better. A white man pretends to be a black woman, because many science fiction readers specifically want to read books authored by a woman of colour, and he wants to cash in on this trend.

A thirty-something male children's author pretended to be a female retired schoolteacher. He reasoned—perhaps rightly—that parents of young children would prefer to buy books written by someone like that. He wanted me to help him deceive readers, penning not only a fictitious author bio, but a weekly blog about the alleged experiences of the retired female teacher. He offered me good money for this.

Perhaps the deception doesn't sound too bad to you. But consider this scenario: The 'female retired schoolteacher' invites children to meet her... and the parents, trusting her because they 'know' her from her wonderful books and her weekly blog, allow this. What if the man turns out to be a paedophile who entraps children this way?

In all those cases, I stuck to my 'no deceit' rule and said no.

A FRIEND'S EXPERIENCE

One of my friends, a writer of Erotic Romance novels, took a job writing for a pornography website. Her personal view was that any kind of sex between consenting adults was fine: if people chose to practice or watch kinky activities, that was their business.

For a year, she wrote product descriptions for adult fetish videos and articles designed to increase sexual desires. The assignment grew into an ongoing, almost full-time job which she enjoyed, and it paid well. She thought she'd landed the perfect client.

Then she discovered that the website was a gateway to another, darker business—one that promoted non-consensual sex (rape). Her copy served to attract people to the 'official' porn site. Once people were hooked on that, the client lured them to the real website, the 'rape' one.

When my friend saw some of what was going on there, she vomited and had nightmares for weeks.

I'm telling you this story so you're aware that even if clients look okay, their business can have a darker side which you may unwittingly support. For big jobs and ongoing work, do your research and find out as much about the client as possible.

NOVICE MISTAKES TO AVOID

Don't let clients trick you into doing their dirty work for them. Some cunning clients hire inexperienced copywriters, giving them at legitimate tasks at first. Then they gradually give you more dodgy assignments, and before you know, you do things you had never meant to. This includes writing fake customer reviews and character testimonials.

INSIDER TIP

If you decide beforehand what you are and are not willing to do, you can see at a glance whether to apply for a job and accept an assignment. It will save you the stress of making moral decisions under pressure.

Whatever your personal values are, uphold them.

NICHOLAS' SUGGESTION

Like Rayne, my ethics include not writing fake reviews. When my best client asked me to do just that, I was torn. On one hand, I didn't want to jeopardise our relationship. On the other, it compromised my ethics.

I respectfully declined, making it clear that I didn't judge them in any way—I know full well that this is common practice. But this is just one I would rather not undertake.

She gave that assignment to someone else but appreciated my candour and gave me more work than ever before—of the kind I was happy to handle.

If a client gets upset at you for respecting your ethics, you're probably better off working for someone else, as Rayne explains in the next chapter.

ASSIGNMENTS

1. Think about your personal values. What matters to you? (For instance, honesty, chastity, temperance, the Ten Commandments, your political affiliations, the environment, the sanctity of marriage, animal welfare....) Write them down. Now imagine what kind of assignment might offend against these values. Define the kind of assignments you will not take.

   Write down your 'will not' principles, either as list or as a single statement. Putting this in writing will confirm your commitment.

2. Visit a site where copywriting jobs are advertised, e.g. Upwork. Study the currently posted job descriptions, and identify the ones which go against your personal ethics. Try to read between the lines, too – is there something the client is only hinting at that could be potentially problematic? This is useful practice for when you start applying for real jobs.

CHAPTER 27

TROUBLESHOOTING: HOW TO DEAL WITH DIFFICULT CLIENTS

Rayne Hall

In every freelancing business, some clients cause trouble, and you need to know how to handle them.

COMMON PROBLEMS

Here are some of the difficulties you are likely to encounter:

- **Clients who don't pay.** If a client misses a scheduled payment once, assume that it's an oversight, and remind them in a friendly way. A good approach is to mention it casually as part of another communication. ("By the way, I see my last invoice hasn't been paid yet.") If the client repeatedly forgets to pay, or delays payment with excuses, you need to be clear and firm. Send a written payment reminder and don't deliver any further work until you have received what you're owed.

- **Clients who expect you to do things you hadn't agreed to.** This can include unethical tasks—such as writing fake customer reviews and testimonials—or simply more work than you agreed for the fixed fee. Remind them of the written agreement, and say "Sorry, I won't do that," or "I can do that, but my fee will increase to XX amount."

- **Clients who don't communicate.** You wait for their instructions, choices or decisions, so you can progress with your work, but they don't answer your questions and ignore your reminders. If a client doesn't communicate, your best approach is to communicate more—and do it in writing. If a client doesn't answer questions, give them a deadline by when you need the information. If their failure to communicate holds up your process, write, "Since I haven't received the promised instructions, I decided to opt for Choice B" and continue your job.

WHAT TO SAY, AND HOW TO SAY IT

Stay calm and courteous. Don't react emotionally. Simply say something like,

"Thanks for our interesting suggestion, but I won't do that."

"You may have forgotten that my fee was due last week. Here are my bank details again."

"I'm sorry, but this is not in my job description."

"May I remind you of what we agreed in our contract?"

"Unless you provide this information today, the advertisement will not be ready on the date you want."

"I'll be happy to undertake this additional task for $300."

It's a good idea to put everything in writing, especially with a potentially troublesome client.

NOVICE MISTAKE TO AVOID

Inexperienced freelancers put up with payment delays, borderline unethical demands, and more, because they are too shy to speak up. Things will get worse because the clients see that they can get away with it. Don't hope that problems will go away. They won't.

INSIDER TIP

At the slightest hint of a problem, bring up the issue in writing. Should matters escalate, you'll be able to document that you have warned the client early on.

NICHOLAS' SUGGESTION

One of the best parts of being a freelancer is that you don't have a boss to answer to.

One of the worst parts of being a freelancer is that you have many clients to answer to.

Over the past 30 years, some 97% of my clients were agreeable, lovely people who were great to work with. Any problems encountered were solved amicably in the ways that Rayne suggests here (*scripta manent*—"written words remain"—is the golden rule here), leaving both parties happy.

The remaining 3% consisted, quite frankly, of sociopaths who either wanted to con me or had an unhealthy need to prove their superiority over anyone unfortunate enough to work for them. Or, as I once asked such a client, "what did your last slave die of?"

In one of the worst cases, I worked for a man who had five secretaries working for him when he hired me. A few months later, only two remained. One had suffered two strokes—she was in her late thirties. Another simply disappeared and never showed up for work again. And a third one quit screaming at her boss, "I'd rather clean stairs than work here anymore."

I now look for warning signs that a client may belong to that 3% group and drop them faster than you can say, "My, what a clean stairway." In my experience, no amount of money can make it worth dealing with such people. Also, they will take up so much of your time and energy that you won't be able to focus on doing a great job for the rest of your clients.

Copywriting

ASSIGNMENT

Talk to a freelancer—not necessarily a copywriter—and find out what kinds of trouble she has experienced with her clients, and how she prevents these problems from escalating. You can learn a lot from other people's difficulties and solutions.

CHAPTER 28

EXPAND YOUR SCOPE: DEVELOPING YOUR BUSINESS

Rayne Hall

Once your copywriting venture is taking off, seek to keep it going and expand it.

REPEAT CLIENTS

Keeping clients is less work than finding new ones. This cuts down on the amount of time you spend on marketing. It also reduces the risks and stresses associated with new clients, i.e. dealing with troublesome people and chasing up delayed payments.

Do what you can to keep your good clients happy, so they will hire you again and again.

ONGOING JOBS

Big companies often hire freelancers on an ongoing basis, for example, for five or 30 hours per week. If you and your client are happy working together, this is an excellent arrangement. It takes away some of the worries about whether you'll make enough money next month to pay the bills.

Make sure you have **a written agreement** that specifies how much work you will do, and how much notice either party must give to terminate the contract.

REFERRALS

When clients are happy with your work, they will recommend you to other clients. This, too, saves marketing time. You can ask your satisfied clients to suggest you to others.

SUBCONTRACTING

Some copywriters form their own agencies, brokering assignments for other freelancers. Yet others—once they get more work than they can handle—hire other copywriters to do the job. Although this can be a lucrative business, it has many pitfalls.

You become responsible for the quality and delivery of the other writers' work—and if they deliver substandard copy or miss deadlines, you're in trouble. Also, a client who discovers that you've subcontracted the job instead of doing it yourself will feel deceived and may not hire you again.

EXPAND THE SCOPE

You can grow your business by providing services in related areas. This can work really well if you target the same clients.

Here are some fields you may be able to incorporate:

- SEO Optimisation
- Social Media Marketing
- Web Design
- Ghostwriting
- Video Script Writing

You can learn those skills gradually while working as a copywriter.

OTHER FORMS OF WRITING

Many copywriters are also novelists, non-fiction authors, journalists or poets. However, it is best to keep these activities separate from your business. Practice your fiction or poetry as a hobby, or as a separate venture.

NOVICE MISTAKES TO AVOID

Don't try to do everything, or you'll end up as a 'Jack of All Trades, Master of None'. Remember, it's best to be a specialist. Once you've mastered the craft of copywriting, add one or two related skills to your portfolio, but don't overdo it. Don't lose focus, or clients won't take you seriously.

INSIDER TIP

Study advertisements on agency sites like Upwork. When clients seek to hire copywriters, which additional services do many of them request as part of the job? Consider learning one of those in-demand skills.

NICHOLAS' SUGGESTION

While I agree with Rayne that a client who discovers that you've subcontracted the job instead of doing it yourself may feel deceived, I often subcontract work. As with everything else, honesty is the best policy here.

An agency I work with recently asked me to write over 100,000 words within a couple of months. A few days later, they offered me an urgent assignment that had just come up. I explained that I'd have to hire some extra writers to complete both projects in time and they were happy to let me do so.

Thankfully, I have certain writers I work with in situations like this, so getting the required help was easy. These people offer an excellent service at a great price. Even so, I made sure that I was the one to approve all copy and handle the hiring process. All the client had to do was approve the copy and pay us.

Clients want to know that the work will be handled professionally, within budget, on time, and without any fuss. They juggle a million things at work and don't need any drama or extra responsibilities. As long as I can ensure all that and I'm honest with my clients, I feel free to hire more people to help me out when necessary.

ASSIGNMENT

Which related field of work would interest you? Research how much demand there is currently for freelancers providing such services. Find out what training opportunities exist.

DEAR READER,

Nicholas and I hope you found these tips helpful and will apply them when you develop your copywriting business.

We'd love it if you could post a review on Amazon or some other book site where you have an account and posting privileges. Maybe you can mention which chapters you found most interesting and helpful, and why.

Email me the link to your review, and I'll send you a free review copy (ebook) of one of my other Writer's Craft books. Let me know which one you would like: *Writing Fight Scenes, Writing Scary Scenes, The Word-Loss Diet, Writing About Magic, Writing About Villains, Writing Dark Stories, Euphonics For Writers, Writing Short Stories to Promote Your Novels, Twitter for Writers, Why Does My Book Not Sell? 20 Simple Fixes, Writing Vivid Settings, How To Train Your Cat To Promote Your Book, Writing Deep Point of View, Getting Book Reviews, Novel Revision Prompts, Writing Vivid Dialogue, Writing Vivid Characters, Writing Book Blurbs and Synopses, Writing Vivid Plots, Write Your Way Out Of Depression: Practical Self-Therapy For Creative Writers, Fantasy Writing Prompts, Horror Writing Prompts, How to Write That Scene, More Horror Writing Prompts, Writing Love Scenes, Author Branding, Fiction Pacing, Ghostwriting, Writing Gothic Fiction.* (For a title list with brief descriptions, see this page on my website: https://www.raynehall.com/books-for-writers).

My email is contact@raynehall.com. Drop me a line if you've spotted any typos which have escaped the proof-reader's eagle eyes, or want to give me private feedback or have questions.

Copywriting

You can also contact me on Twitter: https://twitter.com/RayneHall. Tweet me that you've read this book, and I'll probably follow you back.

If you want to hear from me more often, I have a newsletter with writing tips, mini writing contests, special offers, information about upcoming books, and glimpses into my life in Bulgaria and adventures with my rescue cats. https://forms.aweber.com/form/13/896688713.htm

If you find this book helpful, it would be great if you could spread the word about it. Maybe you know other writers who would benefit.

With best wishes for your copywriting success,

Rayne Hall

ACKNOWLEDGEMENTS

I give sincere thanks to the members of the Professional Authors online group who read the draft chapters and offered valuable feedback.

The book cover is by Erica Syverson and Jasmine Bailey. Monica Bryant-Norved proofread the manuscript, and Eled Cernik formatted the book.

And finally, I say thank you to my sweet cats Sulu, Uhura (Yura) and T'Pau who took turns snuggling on the desk between my arms while I typed.

Rayne Hall

I am grateful to Rayne for the opportunity to work with her on this book. She was one of the first people who advised me when I started writing professionally and I consider her one of my mentors. Naturally, I was tickled pink when she suggested we write this book together. I loved working with her and hope we can continue our collaboration in the future.

I thank God every day for letting me make a living doing something I love. I'm particularly grateful to Laura Williams and everyone at InSync Media for entrusting me with writing and editing their clients' copy. I hope you, the reader, also find such wonderful people to work with!

Nicholas C Rossis

ABOUT THE AUTHORS

Rayne Hall

Rayne Hall writes non-fiction books (including the Writer's Craft series) as well as Gothic Ghost and Horror stories, educational materials and promotional copy for clients.

She lives in rural Bulgaria where she enjoys long walks in the countryside, practices permaculture gardening and trains cats.

Nicholas C Rossis

Nicholas C. Rossis lives to write and does so from his cottage on the edge of a magical forest in Athens, Greece. When not writing copy for his clients, he composes epic fantasies, children's books, and short sci-fi stories, chats with fans and colleagues, writes blog posts, and enjoys the antics of his dog and baby daughter, both of whom claim his lap as home. His books have won numerous awards, including the prestigious IBBY Award (Greece).

www.ingramcontent.com/pod-product-compliance
Lightning Source LLC
Chambersburg PA
CBHW070635220526
45466CB00001B/181